Silver Screen to Digital:
A Brief History of Film Technology

Silver Screen to Digital: A Brief History of Film Technology

Carlo Montanaro

Translated from Italian by
Liam Mac Gabhann

British Library Cataloguing in Publication Data

Silver Screen to Digital:
A Brief History of Film Technology

A catalogue entry for this book is available from the British Library

ISBN: 0 86196 746 9 (Paperback))
ISBN: 0 86196 966 1 (ebook-MOBI)
ISBN: 0 86196 967 8 (ebook-EPUB)
ISBN: 0 86196 968 5 (ebook-EPDF)

The author acknowledges the support of Le Giornate del Cinema Muto which made the publication of this book possible.

The images reproduced in this volume are from Archivio Carlo Montanaro.
Nonetheless, the publishers declare their willingness to respect the rights of the owners of any images herein that could not be contacted during the preparation of this volume.

Published by
John Libbey Publishing Ltd, 205 Crescent Road, New Barnet, Herts EN4 8SB, United Kingdom   e-mail: john.libbey@orange.fr; web site: www.johnlibbey.com

Distributed Worldwide by
Indiana University Press, Herman B Wells Library—350, 1320 E. 10th St., Bloomington, IN 47405, USA. www.iupress.indiana.edu

Printed and bound in the United Kingdom by Latimer-Trend.

Contents

Colour Plates facing page 42

The Author's acknowledgements:
As a child I started to break toys and other things in an attempt to understand "how they worked". Having learned from my father's spankings (the toys were made of tin and I frequently cut my fingers), I soon looked to insiders "in the field" to help me understand. They tried to explain if not the scientific facts, at least the logic behind the phenomena that so intrigued me. To all of them, electricians, mechanics, projectionists and cameramen, cinematographers, specialists and experts in various and varied areas of expertise (my inexhaustible curiosity ...) my deepest thanks: it would be impossible to remember them all. It is easier to name, in the hope of remembering them correctly, my fellow travellers: Gian Piero Brunetta, Angelo Schwarz, Gabriele Coassin, Paolo Gioli, Livio Ricci, Juan Gabriel Tharratz, Camillo Bassotto, Lucio Ramelli, Marie-Hélène Lehérissey Méliès, Laurent Mannoni, Walter Alberti, Gianni Comencini, Riccardo Redi; and, during almost 40 years, all the Board members of Le Giornate del Cinema Muto: Paolo Cherchi Usai, Lorenzo Codelli, Piero Colussi, Andrea Crozzoli, Luciano De Giusti, Livio Jacob, Piera Patat, David Robinson, Davide Turconi, Jay Weissberg – and Jean Mitry, the festival first Honorary President.

Chapter One

In the beginning, there was a man turning a crank

In cinema today it can happen that the credits last as long as a short film. Think of the paradox reached in James Cameron's *Titanic* (1998): a song that was fundamental in promoting the film (it even had its own visionary video-clip) was employed only during the credits, and yet, that song was not long enough for the long list of the people involved in the creation of the film. Moreover, these reviews of cast and technicians mark a break-off point: though the screen is still illuminated the audience prepares to leave. On TV it is viewed as superfluous, something extra to be faded out as soon as possible for a few precious minutes of lucrative advertising. Nevertheless, those names and jobs mark the sum total of the technical and creative minds who, thanks to the producers' financial input, breathe life into the ideas, dreams and vision of a director: the person ultimately responsible for the creation of each and every cinematographic work. The ever-growing importance of "special effects" (though they may not actually be readily visible) has led to a huge increase in the personnel involved and consequently the legal obligation to cite them in the credits. There were no titles or names in the early days of cinema, no need to cite anything, the phenomenon itself merely needed to exist to charm, intrigue and win over ever-increasing audiences. It was a "special effect" in its own right, expanding known concepts of reproduction that had developed over the centuries, each one a genial step forward in technology in its own age, each progressively more refined and more persuasive. For the most part, the first steps were based on drawing, painting and engraving. Then came photogra-

1

phy which became popular even among the lower classes. But the moment photography came to life, literally (consider the the title *La Photographie Animée* chosen in 1899[1] by Eugène Trutat for one of the first books to document cinematography), it changed the way we saw the world for ever.

The first cine-cameras did not stand out particularly. In one extraordinary short Lumière film[2] shot at a pond in a park (*Bassin des Tuileries*, 1896) where some children are playing with toy boats, we see a boy who does not notice the anonymous technician's tripod. He is seen from behind as he enters[3] and stops, his attention focused on the pond, he is first asked verbally to get out of the way, not understanding, he turns around and an umbrella comes from the right side of the screen to push him out towards the left. Today, a child would immediately recognize the camera and would be much more likely to be drawn to it than to his peers at play.

Having still to be codified, the act of filming was imbued with an air of mystery: wooden boxes on a tripod and someone either behind or beside it quickly turning the little crank, and the subsequent projections, in the dark with the rhythmic whiz of turning cogs covered by the clang of a piano. At that time no-one could have predicted the joyous and seemingly chaotic confusion, the alternation of shouting and silence, the heaps of weird and wonderful materials, the switching on and off of huge voltages of light that are essential features of any self-respecting film set. Though we have come to know all its tricks, the intimacy of the cinema theatre, the true temple of our collective imagination, has lost nothing of its spell. We are still enchanted by its lifelike portrayals, of any possible place, emotion and situation, an endless replica of life and death, love and hate, picaresque adventures acting as interior analysis. At the very first screenings in the underground

1 Bibliothèque Photographique – Eug. Trutat *La Photographie Animée*, Paris, Gauthier-Villars, Imprimeur-Libraire, 1899.

2 Sous la direction de Michelle Aubert, Jean-Claude Seguin, *La Production Cinématographique des Frères Lumières*, Bibliothèque du Film (BIFI) Editions Mémoires de Cinéma, 1996, p. 234.

3 When filming to "enter" or "exit" have acquired the meaning of appearing or leaving the scene from the perspective of the camera: thus "enter" means coming in towards the centre or the screen and "exit" is going in the opposite direction, towards the borders of the shot.

rooms of the Grand Café, the *Salon Indien* hastily and exotically decorated to justify the somewhat expensive 1 franc ticket, each film began with the frozen image of the first frame, leading the spectators to fear they were to be bamboozled by yet another magic lantern show[4] only to be completely amazed seeing "life as it is". But it has been technique that has gradually enabled cine-matographers to broaden their horizon, it is the foundation for any other technological system that furthers the capacity to capture shreds of reality and transform them into emotion.

---

4   Georges Méliès was present at the screening: *"I and the other invitees found ourselves before a small screen like those used for Molteni projections, and after a few moments a motionless photograph appeared showing Place Bellcour in Lion* [sic]*. Somewhat surprised, I had just enough time to remark to the person next to me: They have brought us here for some projections, I've being doing that for over ten years. I had not even finished when a horse drawing a carriage began to march towards us, followed by other vehicles, passers-by, and in short, all the activity of the street. We were speechless, absolutely amazed, overcome by indescribable surprise."* Cited in Bernard Chardère, Guy et Marjorie Borgé, *Les Lumières*, Payot, Lausanne-Bibliothèque des Arts, Paris 1985, p. 96.

Chapter Two

The invention of celluloid and the first hunters of moving images

It had all begun just a few years earlier and in a much more perfunctory manner. Many in Europe endeavoured to make moving photography a reality, yet, though they came close, for one reason or another, they were unable. Meanwhile, in America, attempting to match what he had already achieved in sound (the phonograph), Thomas Alva Edison deposited a *caveat* (a provisional patent application) on October 8, 1888 hypothesising a series of continuous photographic images taken *at intervals*, analogous to his machine that reproduced sound. He then entrusted the research to the Englishman William Kennedy-Laurie Dickson. Dickson worked at the West Orange laboratories, refining and adapting scientific and technological discoveries that were widely known, if not already commercialised (optical instruments, toys and photography). However he also researched new ways forward linked to other equipment, for example, the phonograph. Research into movement analysis was already in progress on both continents. Eadweard Muybridge and Étienne-Jules Marey had demonstrated how it was possible not only to capture and reproduce the intermediate phases of human and animal movements, and then print them in multiple copies, but also how to create spectacular, composite syntheses. It is symptomatic, however, that for Muybridge's *Zoopraxiscope* each photograph needed to be drawn with proportional adjustments to ensure a correct reproduction during projection, compensating for the slight *anamorphosis* that would otherwise be perceived because of its rotating shutter. But Muybridge and Marey could only adapt to the limits of photography at that time. To highlight the bodies of their models they used *shots* where backgrounds were necessarily dark, a compromise between photographic studio and theatre. Indeed, the photographic emulsion hardly reacted with the red end of the spectrum[5] and there was very little sensitivity all round. The Lumières' highly successful industrial "blue label"[6] plates dated 1890, would be calculated today at 4 ASA.[7] Consequently, as a lot of light was needed it was only possible to photograph in full sunlight, lens luminosity was still low, but first and foremost artificial lighting was based on a glow, on that reddish light that created little exposure. However, the trigger that provided the impetus to Dickson's research at that moment in history was the invention of celluloid. Celluloid, an antecedent of the infinite varieties of contemporary plastic, is organic; it is made of a mixture of nitrocellulose[8] and camphor. Since 1869, it has been used for the most diverse purposes, substituting glass and paper. Thanks to the intuition of George Eastman[9] in 1889, it became the support par excellence for photography for all: "You press the button, We do the rest". The fact that celluloid was also highly inflammable, in critical conditions even self-deflagrating, was one of the many prices to be paid for scientific, technological and industrial progress.

However, another transparent and flexible material was already found in a patent (applied for on December 1, 1888 and granted on January 14, 1889) by Emile Reynaud for his Théâtre Optique:

> His apparatus aimed at creating the illusion of movement, but no longer limited to rotating repetition [...] obtaining, on the contrary, indefinite variety and duration, thus producing realistic and unlimited scenes [...]. The

5   Indeed, initially, even green and yellow light had little effect on the emulsion.

6   Société Antoine Lumière et Fils located in Lyon.

7   A system to determine the sensitivity of photographic emulsions introduced in America (American Standards Association) in 1943 similar to DIN (Deutsche Industrie Normen) already in use in Europe as of 1931. Since the 70s a new standard is in use (ISO: International Standard Organization) unifying the two earlier standards on a global level.

8   Used in photography and cinema until the fifties, "nitrate" is dangerous to handle but possesses a crystalline transparency that has never been equalled by any of its safer replacements (acetate, triacetate, polyester) adopted by manufacturers.

9   In actual fact, it is known that others, in particular John Carbutt and Hannibal Goodwin, had already considered celluloid as a support for photographic film. However, it was Eastman who understood how to move on to the industrial phase.

innovative method consisted in a devices creating the illusion of movement through a flexible strip of indefinite length with a series of successive poses rolled from reel to reel across the crown of the instrument which allowed for projection. The poses could be drawn by hand or printed using any reproduction procedure, in black or colour, or obtained from nature through photography.[10]

While Edison's contemporary application described a "moving vision obtained" with photography "in the same way that sound is recorded on a phonograph", it is very clear that Reynaud's intuition was far more concrete and prophetic. This is hardly the place to settle the many outstanding disputes on the paternity of various patents and/or technological systems; they will probably remain forever unsolved. Nonetheless, with the invention and of his Théâtre Optique Reynaud crossed what we can call a point of no return. He used a substance known as crystalloid (a somewhat fragile gelatin chemically related to celluloid) cut into squares, assembled in strips and wound onto reels (spools, analogous to those used in spinning). These were wound thanks to central perforations between the images which engaged with metal pins protruding from the crown (the large central rotating drum with mirrors set inside)[11] drawing it along while keeping each drawing perfectly in line, a continuous and indefinite flow for as long as was necessary to unroll the complete strip. The story could now last as long as its creator decided: 700 poses, 50 meters long, for example, in *A bon bock* (the first "comic scene" dated 1892, unfortunately destroyed) or 636 images, 45 meters, for *Autour d'une cabine* from 1893–94 and lasting about fifteen minutes (the most famous because it is exists complete). The cyclic repetition typical of optical toys had been definitively left behind and likewise the static lantern show and its changing sets of rectangular slides. Analogous to the latest innovations of the Magic Lantern (double and triple lanterns for cross-fading effects) and the Praxinoscope

10 Vv.Aa. *Les maîtres du cinéma, Emile Reynaud peintre de films 1844–1918*, Cinémathèque Française, Paris, 1945 p. 58.

11 Like the Praxinoscope, the heart of the Théâtre Optique was a prism of mirrors. This alternating vision in the rotation compared to the continuous motion of the reflecting support was later also used for normal projection, but the system (subsequently transformed with reflecting crystal prisms) was abandoned at the turn of the 40s. It is a technology still employed in moviolas and high speed cameras used for slow motion.

Theatre where a printed background was semi-reflected on a transparent crystal, the Théâtre Optique created its setting by using two overlapping light sources. One lantern provided the background scene painted on glass, while the other projected the vignettes (*poses*) with a dense black background blocking the passage of light around the brightly coloured characters on the crystalloid. These two sources were integrated in rear-screen projection. This blending of *mattes* and the dynamic performance of actors against an added backdrop, initially through multiple exposures of the same negative and later through refined overprinting, is a fundamental principle not only of photographic manipulation, but also, and above all, of the *special effects* in cinema. What matters most however, is that, beyond the virtuality achieved through drawings,[12] Reynaud foreshadowed the possibility of applying the same procedures to photographic images. But it was precisely the adoption of another strip of emulsified and perforated celluloid – almost immediately considered just the right width at 35mm – that was the key to bringing Reynaud's *natural* intuition on to the next stage.

---

12 Though many consider it the precursor of animation, in actual fact, Reynaud was only making a virtue of necessity...

Chapter Three

Thomas A. Edison: from the Kinetograph to the Kinetoscope

This of course leads us to Edison. On his famous visit to the 1889 World Exhibition in Paris, Edison acquired a wealth of information including a "guided tour" with Marey whose Chronophotography had already captured a series of successive *poses* on Eastman's paper film (which, unfortunately, had not yet been perforated). Moreover, the studies of the German physiologist Hermann von Helmholtz changed the logic of his research,[13] henceforth he considered it indispensable to base his experiments on 46 frames per second. This, and more besides, was written into a new *caveat* dated 2 November, 1889 and in a subsequent patent for a filming device – the Kinetograph – filed on 24 August, 1891 but not registered until 31 August, 1897. Not forgetting his initial idea of coupling sound and image (obtained by synchronising two separate devices), the project now envisioned a camera with a 50 foot horizontal scroll of emulsified celluloid with regular perforations only on one side. These holes (4 per frame) would allow the film to run regularly with equally regular periodic interruptions (not considered essential in the patent) thanks to a snap mechanism which presumably, from the outset, consisted of two perpendicular cogs. Presumably, because, though this is the apparatus described in the patent, the definitive mechanical structure was afforded a margin of modification over six whole

---

13 According to von Helmholtz the human eye could not perceive the difference between continuous light and a series of electric sparks at a rate of about 50 per second. But we will see that that created problems only during projection, and Edison at that time, given his entrepreneurial vision, was not excessively interested in projection.

years of trials (an indication of the persuasive skill of a super entrepreneur such as Edison in influencing the competent authorities). But, again, let us leave aside speculation and controversy. Because this was not actually the winning system in the long run; it only the first one able to function – though in an approximate manner. While filming, which was problematic due to the high speed required and the poor sensitivity of the emulsion, reached plausible though not encouraging results, it was the complementary phase, *viewing*, though less complex and therefore patented sooner (within a couple of years: March 14, 1893), that turned out to be a complete failure. The viewing device was the Kinetoscope, activated by inserting a coin, it allowed for just one spectator at a time and ran (like the Kinetograph) on electricity. Other assessments aside, we might hypothesise that the decision to commercialise the system depended largely on the initial idea of including *sound*, sooner or later. Indeed, in 1895, about fifty Kinetophones were manufactured, these included an *audio* cylinder that could be heard through rubber earphones while the spectator peered into the peephole. With the technology of the time it was possible (however precariously) to match a sound recording on a phonograph with the Kinetograph, through electromagnetic synchronism (everything ran on electricity), what was not possible however was *amplification* – making the sound audible for more than ten people. It was better, therefore, to aim for an immediate return on the investment through individual viewings, also because adding sound remained part of the hypothesis. Given the multiplicity of films, these personal viewings obviously needed as many devices as there were subjects to be viewed.

In retrospect, we now known that there were other erroneous assessments in Edison's invention and exploitation of animated photography. The absence of patents outside the United States allowed his agents (in particular Robert William Paul in Great Britain) to illegally replicate the Kinetoscope (the only machine on the market sold together with the films). Moreover, they made independent improvements, producing variations – especially in filming – thus autonomously broaden the choice of films available to consumers. There was the idea of a show within the show (dancers, jugglers, boxers, etc.) in the choice of *subjects* filmed against a sort of blind proscenium (a black background needed to highlight the activity) which could then be resold, miniaturised yet realistic, beyond the eyepiece of the Kinetoscope. Objectively, it was difficult to imagine transferring the complex, rudimentary apparatus, weighed down by its electrical generator, out of its first, decidedly primitive studio (the Black Maria – rotatable to control sunlight and made of soundproofing materials for recording). Nevertheless, lacking in competition, and therefore any opportunity to emulate something different, the Kinetograph and Kinetoscope, despite all their limitations, initiated brief but intense period of glory.

Chapter Four

The invention of the Cinématographe Lumière

The first commercial presentation at the Cinématographe Lumière marks the official date of the birth of cinema. On Saturday, December 28, 1895, following a long labour that had involved, and continued to involve, dozens of craftsmen from the most diverse fields (lanternists, pharmacists, photographers, inventors and others), two industrialists with some absolutely original innovations managed to draw together the best from all previous experiments. They have been consecrated as the inventors of cinema. Recent writers have highlighted the unscrupulous manner in which Louis and Auguste Lumière employed and re-elaborated other people's insights and conclusions.[14] Nonetheless, one fact cannot be denied: their Cinématographe was the simplest and most functional device capable of solving the problems related to "animated photography" – attaining, much like today's multi-billion dollar productions, the maximum result with the minimum effort. It was conceived not only for *filming* but also, and above all, for *projection* – and for groups of viewers, not single individuals. By replacing some accessories, this transferable quality also allowed for the equally important and fundamental intermediate phase of copy printing in an equally simple and functional manner. Furthermore, it's used a kind of *claw*[15] which, though modified and perfected, is still used today and remains at the heart of every film camera. A different mechanism was to take over in

14 Cf Laurent Mannoni, Marc de Ferrière le Vayer and Paul Demeny, *Georges Demenÿ, pionnier du cinéma*, PAGINE éditions, 1997.

15 What appears to have been the very first Cinématographe, based on sensitised paper bands, used tweezers, a system that was soon abandoned at the time of the first patent on 13 February, 1895 (see *La production cinématographique...*, cit., p. 15).

projectors as we will see later: the *Maltese Cross*. What remained in common with Edison was the film (35mm wide and about 17 meters long) and the idea of perforation: the Lumière *holes* were round with just one on either side of the frame (maintaining compatibility with Edison's 4 + 4 , but just engaging two at a time). Otherwise, everything was different, starting from the mechanism, which was operated manually, and the lower frame rate – from Edison's original 46 frames in the Kinetoscope to 16 frames per second (fps), in the mechanical terms it was two turns of the good old crank. While during the filming phase this yielded a shot three times longer form the same length of film stock, projection was marred by an annoying *flicker* since the spectator was completely aware of the shutter interrupting the light between each frame. It was to take many efforts over several years to understand how to reconcile the scientific necessity (48–50 fps) with film shot at slower speeds: it was sufficient to fit the shutter with two more vanes, thus interrupting the light even when the frame was not actually changing, this creating the impression of a faster frame rate. The result was both intuitive and mathematical: three vanes in a projector at 16 fps yielded a total of 48 interruptions. As of 1902,[16] flicker disappeared, allowing, among other things, for the gradual extension of projection times from the initial composite formula (in the sense of a broad range of subjects) to the current dimension of the *feature film*,[17] no longer wearing out the eyes of the enthusiastic audience. Electrification and sound were not part of the initial concept of the Cinématographe. It was perfectly suited for recording "life as it is" anywhere, outdoors, and in any situation that could be managed using normal natural light.

There was no film studios based on the photographic studio, therefore, only whatever self-contained *action* was possible in the fifty seconds of autonomy granted by a length of film. A precise, productive awareness of these limits can be seen in Lumière productions. Starting from the very first works, especially *Employees*

---

16   According to the memoirs of Oskar Messter, this invention was developed in 1901 by one Theodor Pätzold who put it into use as of 1902: cf. Riccardo Redi, "Tecnologia rivisitata", in Antonio Costa (edited by), *La meccanica del visibile*, La Casa Usher, Florence 1983, p. 40.

17   According to Italian law (no. 1213 of 1965, though it is constantly adjusted over time), the length of a short film is set at no less than 290 m. and that of a feature film is above 1600 m.

Leaving the Lumière Factory (which exists in as many as four different versions – which one was shown on March 22, 1895?) showing the complete workforce, male and female, leaving the Lumière factory in what is today rue Premier Film. In all probability the scene had been rehearsed, and though the Lumière films retain the flavour of current events, it is not difficult to find, within many of them, the need for a certain amount of minimal but realistic *staging* so as to lend a conclusive logic to the action, as far as possible.[18] Though we cannot possibly imagine[19] the effect these first screenings had on the spectators, the immediate, universal enthusiasm that greeted the international tours managed by the associates[20] of the Lumière organisation is hardly surprisingly. This led to a quick reconversion of other systems in use. The Edison Company *in primis* purchased and recycled a projector developed by Thomas Armat and Charles Francis Jenkins (1896), under the name Vitascope[21] and, besides privileging outdoor shooting, began to propose screening to a ever wider audiences.

18 See, for example, the set of *films* shot in Venice, where the same characters, the same gondola and the same gondolier are used to animate the most important backgrounds, from St. Mark's Square to the Grand Canal and Rialto.

19 Despite dozens and dozens of contemporary accounts, since we have always been immersed in moving images, for us a world without this form of information and entertainment it is unthinkable!

20 One fact that should not be overlooked when considering the ease with which these tours were organised is the Lumières' pre-existing commercial network, aided by their membership of the freemasonry which, ethical or moral issues aside, though it may not have imposed relations among members, it certainly favoured them.

21 In fact, Armat and Jenkins' Phantoscope had been in operation since September 1895, projecting Edison films made for the Kinetoscope. Only in April 1896 did Raff and Gammon of Edison's Kinetoscope Company acquire the exclusive rights to this machine, which was renamed Vitascope and passed off as an Edison invention. For the record, on August 28, 1895, Jenkins and Armat had applied for a patent but it was not registered until July 20, 1897.

Chapter Five

Méliès and the Wonderbox

It is well known that one fundamental "first time" was that of Georges Méliès who was invited to the preview as a friend of the Antoine Lumière, the brothers' father (the organiser of the first public screening). Méliès grasped the potential of this new invention immediately, having dedicated his life to the entertainment of others, managing magic performances and wonders in his theatre.[22] And when Lumières refused to sell him their equipment,[23] he converted a projector into a film camera (the Teatrograph No. 2, Mark 1), bought in England a few months later from the "infidel" (from Edison's perspective) William Paul. He made his debut redoing scenes that had already been filmed as if it were somehow fundamental, as in an exorcism, to understand that he was capable of doing what others had already done.[24] And then, the accident occurred![25] The camera jammed, breaking practically the only rule for cameramen at that time: keep turning the crank until all the film is used. The random *splicing*[26] that ensued caused

22 Méliès had purchased the theatre from the widow of the famous Jean-Eugène Robert-Houdin, the inventor, among other things, of "modern" conjuring.

23 It was not until 1897 that film cameras and films, also with Edison perforations, were commercially marketed.

24 Initially, many "primitive" filmmakers did likewise by necessity: playing card games, getting "their" trains to arrive and whatever else ... .

25 The film, *Place de la Concorde*, dated 1896, n. 54 in the Méliès Catalogue, has yet to be found.

26 The term "stop trick" or "substitution trick" identifies the effect, whereas, in French the description is more pragmatic: *arrêt de camera*. Historically there is one illustrious, existing precedent produced by Edison: *The Execution of Mary Queen of Scots* (28 August, 1895) by Alfred Clark, but the *decapitation effect* obtained by substituting the actress with a mannequin appears somewhat naive. Moreover, it does not lead, as in Méliès' case, to subsequent, creative and continuous use of the technique. A systematic use of the substitution splice (one change per frame) is the principle of one of cinema's purest *genres*: animated film.

two similar objects to be switched in the same position, an omnibus and a hearse (needless to say very different in their meaning), and triggered wonder and laughter. A new, authentic, definitive awareness of the instrument's potential was thus discovered. Filming could stop and restart without the spectator's knowledge, cinema could create a different timeframe from reality. It is still the underlying concept behind editing: each interruption involves subsequent improvements on the negative, through cutting, choosing, eliminating and splicing. But this awareness goes far beyond. In the theatre, magic tricks (appearances, disappearances, materialisations, exchanges of characters) could be executed through simple but effective machinery involving of ropes, trapdoors and lights. *Replacement*, the first and most fundamental of cinematographic tricks, can usually be achieved without any machinery. This is how *make believe* made its grand entrance in the world of cinema, alongside "life as it is". To verify this intuition, Méliès filmed *l'Escamotage d'une dame chez Robert-Houdin*,[27] already a celebrated number at his theatre. But he filmed it outdoors against a painted set between two trees. It showed the transformation of a woman into a skeleton – simply by stopping the camera he eliminated the otherwise indispensable trapdoor. Simply? Not exactly. From the outset, Méliès, like the Lumière brothers, paid great attention to form and composition. Nevertheless, in this case, one cannot but be amazed by the excellent handling of the action and control in the positioning of bodies and objects. Méliès understood that he could revitalise the typical tricks of the theatre, even at this very basic stage. Setting up his camera in the best possible position (the Royal box in Italian theatres), the automatic perspective any optician, photographer or filmmaker would choose, he filmed, reworked and reinvented a scene that had been otherwise codified.

Thus, it became possible to interact with a real image of one's double instead of a disguised accomplice; or likewise, to lose anatomical pieces and not life-like fakes (as in a puppet theatre);

---

27 Interpreted by Méliès himself with Jehanne d'Alcy (born Charlotte Faës, first his lover, then his second wife and finally his widow and custodian of his memories and documents) in 1896, n. 70 of the Catalogue, 20 meters, and still preserved. It is curious that the name of the theatre appears in the title, proudly reaffirming the origin of the trick and the film, which even takes on self-promotional value when Méliès begins to sell his films.

and to visibly alter the dimensions of characters or backgrounds. We know that in photography the principles of these primitive *special effects* were well known and described in technical manuals. We also know that multiple exposures, either against a black background or by masking part of the image had become relatively widespread thanks to the perfection of Magic Lantern shows (including dwarfs and giants), using fading and overlapping images from several projectors;[28] photographs were being used like this with growing frequency. We even know that would-be mediums used pre-exposed plates with vague and fuzzy images to show naive and desperate people the ectoplasmic apparitions of their deceased relatives. So, do we want to get moving? Do we want to create fantastic illusions that manage to defy logic, even if set against a schematic painted backdrop?

Méliès then built a workshop bringing together the attention to light of a photographic studio (a glass roof with white curtains to regulate the intensity of sunlight), his knowledge the theatre (a stage with trapdoors, mobile scaffolding, rigging and balconies) and the emerging needs of cinema (a *dark chamber* as a permanent housing for the camera). Moreover, he added spaces for tailoring, stagecraft, dressing rooms and storage. He became self-sufficient in the design, creation, in-house projection and also the sale of works that replicated theatrical practice. Whether farce, illusion, historical re-enactment or even the reconstruction of contemporary events, everything was filtered through the logic of the theatre, enhanced by photographic manipulation in filming and editing the negative (cutting, choosing, pasting) before printing copies. In some cases printing allowed for further effects by simply over-lapping portions of film in cross fades.

Little seemed to have changed in theatres, therefore, when they began to host the cinematograph as an "attraction", the curtain no longer went up on a stage set but flaunted a flat, white sheet where a similar environment was artificially recreated by the projector. From a conceptual point of view Instead, everything had changed: what was reproduced through that beam of light was

---

28 Unlike the Lantern shows, however, these effects had to appear in the positive copy, since they could not be achieved with multiple projectors.

more synthetic, changed rapidly and allowed otherwise impossible stories to be viewed. But, most importantly, it was reality that had been made equally spectacular.

Chapter Six

Machines and mechanisms

The contrast between representation and reality was the fundamental element that was, gradually and laboriously, to lead to a linguistic growth and the elaboration of the basic elements of cinematographic grammar. But what an effort it was! Once the exorcisms had been dealt with, new prejudices rooted in the simulation of events in scenographic or theatrical environments had to be shaken off.

But let's not get ahead of ourselves. Instead, let us try to feel what it was like to attend one of those first cinematographic shows. Between the end of the nineteenth and the beginning of the twentieth century they began to attract ever wider and more popular audiences – though, after an initial "scientific" enthusiasm, the more educated bourgeoisie, not being inclined to mingle with the lower classes, snubbed them for a long time. We might find ourselves at a pavilion in an amusement park, attracted by colourful bulbs and decorations lighting up the night. The continuous, dull rumble, the smell of petrol and exhaust fumes tell us there is a generator producing electricity for the decorations and projector (a carbon arc lamp and an electric motor) located in front of the screen inside. We might, instead, take our seat in a theatre, in which case, the screen (or *diaphragm*, as it was called then) filled the proscenium and glistened because, as there was no *projection booth*, projection was rear-screen from the back of the stage: to make the image clearer, the white cloth had to be constantly sprayed with water and glycerine to increase its transparency. In this case, however, rather than using electricity the light more likely burned *oxy-hydrogen* or the very dangerous *oxygen and ether*.[29] There was no discernible distinction except for an annoying sparkle that pulsated on the screen. The projector, in this case, was still operated by turning a crank manually. Outside, there was likely to be a barker (as happened in Venice)[30] to attract us: "Oh how fine, how fine!... Oh what great drama! Oh how magnificent! What a show!... Oh! What show! Oh, what drama!". The barker would then move into the hall to describe and comment on the images, speaking over a piano accompaniment. And the show, which would last half an hour at the most, so as not to tire the spectators' eyes, would be a mixture of "reality" and fiction. We might watch a Historical Regatta with several boats that had been coloured by hand; along with this, maybe, a *panorama*, one of those *subjective*[31] ones which, starting from *Panorama du Grand Canal pris d'un bateau* filmed by Alexandre Promio,[32] offering not only sumptuous visions of historical sites but also, and above all, passages through dark mountain tunnels, vertiginous views from cliffs or exotic rivers. Or make-believe, with perhaps a mul-tiplied Méliès as in *L'homme orchestra* or flying as in *L'homme mouche* where he started using the camera vertically (always editing admirably).[33] For years the grand finale was often yet another viewing of the ever exciting – despite the fact that time had assuaged any fear that the locomotive could really enter the room

29 It was highly inflammable ether in a Joly-Normandin projector that caused the fire at the Bazar de la Charithé on May 4, 1897. The accident cost hundreds of lives and, for a moment, questioned the very future of a cinema which was dramatically accused of being the murderer.

30 Gino Bertolini *Italy II – L'ambiente fisico e psichico – Storia sociale del secolo ventesimo,* Istituto Veneto di Arti Grafiche Editore, Venice 1912, p. 161.

31 A shot that simulates the character's perspective and allows the viewer to see it with their own eyes and thus empathise fully, but also one that can objectively describe a deep emotional state. Those first short one-shot films, as we will see, were called a "phantom ride".

32 Alongside *Panorama de la place Saint-Marc pris d'un bateau* (1251 and 1252 respectively in the Lumière Catalogue) filmed in the second half of 1896, it appears to be the first *traveling shot* from a self-propelled vehicle. It seems, however, that another Lumière operator, Constant Girel had had the same the idea and filmed a *Panorama pris d'un bateau* in Cologne only a few weeks earlier (September instead of October). However, this is one of those disputes that cannot be solved, and we are cheering for Venice. see: *La production cinématographique …*, cit., p. 46.

33 By placing the camera perpendicular to the walking surface on an otherwise suspended scene allowed the law of gravity to seem altered.

– *Arrival of a Train at La Ciotat*[34] by Lumière, or one of the many subsequent imitations.

Projectors, however, were no longer those multi-functional Lumière Cinématographes, which, if they continued to be used at all, were only used for filming. Reversible equipment (like the one built by Henri Joly for Charles Pathé in 1895) had, in fact, quickly disappeared from the market. Because, though experiments continued (regardless of those who sought a completely independent path such as Le Prince, Friese-Greene, Skladanovski and others),[35] the true path was already becoming clear: to create *subjects* for the Kinetoscope, beyond Edison's exclusive rights, and to cater for group screenings instead of individual viewings, as had already been the case for Magic Lantern shows for more than a couple of centuries. This implied having on one hand a camera, and on the other projector: two totally independent devices.

In these initial devices two mechanisms worked alongside the Lumière brothers' *claw* to carry out the alternative actions of filming and projection. Georges Demenÿ's *eccentric cam* slid (or better: pulled) the film forward by one frame with each turn without a need for perforations. It was initially designed to obtain negatives for the Phonoscope (one of the pre-cinematographic devices derived from Marey's studies – Demenÿ was his closest collaborator). When Demenÿ joined Léon Gaumont, an up-and-coming young industrialist, the *cam-and-claw* became central to the mechanisms for both filming and projection at the rising Gaumont Film Company – it was abandoned when found to be unreliable. The other mechanism was the *Maltese Cross*,[36] derived from the *Geneva cross* which was well known to watchmakers and had already become part of the world of "magical visions" as the principle of the latest and most ingenious accessory for the Magic Lantern. In 1866, English optician John Beale had built the

34 Various *Arrivée* films were made and not only at La Ciotat station, a couple are not even inventoried in the Lumière Catalogue.

35 It is not useful to retrace the, often brilliant though unfortunate, experiences of those precursors who did not actually contribute to the technical or linguistic advancement of cinema.

36 On issues related to the adoption of the Maltese cross, see, among others, Mario Calzini Cento anni di cinema al cinema, edited by ANEC, 1995 p. 142, 143.

Choreutoscope: a long narrow glass on which a skeleton was drawn in six successive positions. Turning a handle, a ratchet on a metal disk engaged a groove in the mobile wooden frame that held the glass, obtaining rapid, proportional and progressive movement. A horizontal, intermittent shift therefore, and thanks to the speed of projection the sequence of six drawings against a black background created the impression that the skeleton on the screen was being dismembered. The *Geneva Cross* was born, instead, for an intermittent but rotary movement which was therefore continuous. In its primitive form it had already been used in the pre-cinema era (for example the Janssen photographic revolver or Anschülz's Electrotachyscope) and by increasing the number of shots possible at each turn, it soon became one of the most commonly used devices in reversible models, and in the first cameras and projectors. It finally took on the shape it still has today, four slotted arms which, commanded by the eccentric cam, allow a sprocket to drag one frame at each quarter turn. To contain friction and consequent dilatation, the *Maltese Cross* was almost immediately set inside a container full of oil. Ultimately, In the division of labour the *claw* remains the heart of every camera, since it is very precise mechanically yet manageable in a relatively simple way. Moreover, the time the camera is engaged on the set is rather short, any one take hardly ever exceeds two or three minutes, though it is the fruit long and intense periods of positioning, lighting and tests. Shooting a fiction film, the average daily consumption of negative rarely exceeds 1000 meters, i.e. just over 30 minutes of actual footage, which is reduced to between five and ten minutes of material in the pre-assembly selection.

Meanwhile, in projectors the same function continues to be entrusted to the *Maltese Cross*, being more robust in design and material. Indeed, projectors are subject to considerable daily wear since they can operate, uninterrupted, for up to almost two and a half hours of non-stop motion (4000 meters), this can be repeated several times a day, after rewinding. Indeed, the latest technology, the horizontal *rotating platter system* even allows a continuous cycle of projections, and in the most recent multiplexes, can involve more projectors and more screens almost contemporaneously, carefully transferring a single copy from one booth to another.

Chapter Seven

On and off screen

But let us return for a moment to that hall, whether fixed or itinerant, in the early days of cinema. The audience of that time certainly could hardly have noticed what the shrewd eyes of today's cinema goer observes: the perceptible signs in various shots of what was around or even facing the scene being filmed. Naturally, we are not referring to very naive early films: theatre-like scenery, painted wings, canvas or plywood panoramas, with typical trompe-l'oeil shading to create a third dimension; or the first miniature scale models, silhouettes of ships cut out of real photographs and nailed onto small pieces of wood floating on a tank of water with pinches of gunpowder and backgrounds of plaster or papier-mâché, to recreate the atmosphere of naval battles.[37] While we may smile today at such images, we often forget that technological development is gradual, the best that could be attained at one time is ineluctably destined to be perfected and improved. Just as today no one would dream of crossing a desert in a Ford model T, while still recognising that car as the ancestor of all subsequent vehicles, likewise it would be small-minded to ridicule the fame of those first, often crude, rudimentary, and even far-fetched examples of "animated photography" that fascinated our grandparents.

Nevertheless, as we said, the watchful eye of today's audience can sense the oddity of what was fixed forever on the film and what it tells us about how and where filmmakers operated, and moreover, what was excluded or cut from the shot. It is that *off screen* that

37 We are describing one of the first "reenacted news" items, *The Battle of Manila Bay* (33 seconds in length), filmed by J. Stuart Blackton and Albert E. Smith for their American Vitagraph Company on the terrace of a New York building in May 1898 and distributed by the Edison Manufacturing Company This very short film can be seen in *Silver Shadows* dated 1938, Blackton's autobiographical documentary, an eloquent, extraordinary, *making of* with the authors using a cigar to "set off the powders" simulating shots and explosions.

is so important today, not only for the *special effects* (especially animatronics, mechanical *puppets* humanoids or monsters, moved by cables, wires etc.) but also for the correct composition of each image. Think, for example, of notable differences in stature between two actors. In full shots it is impossible not to notice, if the two characters converse in a close up, the shorter is raised, albeit slightly, on a wooden stand (along with other equipment and specific objects, these are the responsibility of the grip team) so as to make the difference in height between the two faces still clear but less accentuated; this stand must, of course, remain *off screen*, outside the space that is caught on film. Evidence of the off-screen world that can be noticed in the cinema of the past might be parts of metal structures making up the glass roofs of the first studios which were sometimes built on rather large surfaces; or different shadows that might even allow you to figure out, albeit roughly, the time of day when the scene was shot; or reflections on surfaces (windows, furniture, or wet items etc.) showing what is in front of the set: the cameraman, the director giving orders etc.

However, *off screen* can also be an linguistic device, ever since 1903 when the English director Robert William Paul used it in *A Chess Dispute*: a single shot in which two Chess players scuffle and fall to the ground, disappearing from sight. The fight continues with arms and heads appearing from below the screen alternately and more and more energetically, until both the contenders "re-appear", disheveled and beaten. Though they do not appear on screen, there is no need to describe the activities of the collaborators that help the two wrestling actors to gradually show the effect of their fight (today we call them the make-up artist and the costume standby). Not everything needs to be included in the shot, therefore it can be tampered with, altered to attain effects which do not always need to be fantastic or unusual, sometimes they can be otherwise unfeasible realistic effects, for example the equipment used for artificial rain or snow. Sometimes, instead, it is simply the microphone that *enters* the field of vision, either because the camera man was distracted or the throw ratio was mistaken. Since we are here, let us introduce another important concept related to *special effects*. In describing typical systems that allow cinema to play with the impossible, whether realistic or not, we have already mentioned double exposures and the matte. Combining these expedients with the certainty of the field of vision (the camera angle and the perspective that automatically derives from it), up until about a decade ago it was only possible to *cover up*, or physically hide such unwanted items with scenery or the use of masses, more or less dense groups of extras (in Roman cinematographic jargon the word used was *impallare*, literally to snooker), or to overlap the same negative with successive shots of drawings, models and so on. And if technology has developed ever more complex and realistic systems over the years to achieve these results (matte and counter-matte, also the "mobile" matte), the principle of *covering up* has only recently been coupled with the much more decisive, revolutionary technique of *removal*, which will soon become the only feasible technique, thanks to the quality of the definition it produces. *Removal* is one of the most extraordinary uses of manipulation of images thanks to digitization and the use of computer technology in cinema (it has been possible since the mid-80s, but only in television).[38] However we running ahead a bit too much.

---

38 Television can control both the brightness (*luma-key*) and the three basic colours (red, green and blue) of the spectrum *(chroma-key)*; the computerised management of images uses these technological expedients systematically.

Chapter Eight

Work on the set. The birth of montage and the discovery of the film set

S
o let us imagine entering one of those almost always glazed film studios that were appearing all around the world, bearing witness the industrialisation of cinema. Compared to Méliès' small studio in Montreuil – at the time a Parisian suburbs – the only real, structural difference was the addition of a technological department for film processing.[39] In the words of Aldo Bernardini:

> [...] each establishment tended to be self-sufficient, i.e. it dealt with the entire production cycle: from shooting to the finished product. Other departments were reserved for the various procedures: printing positives, montage, colouring and toning, etc[40] ...

Only sunlight could be used for filming for at least the first fifteen years, except for a few basically irrelevant, attempts at employing arc lamps (in particular, and this was quite a surprise, in Tsarist Russia). As we have seen, this light came through roofs and glass walls (which also provided protection from bad weather). Full sunlight was filtered through white cotton curtains creating a softer luminescence that attenuated excessively sharp contrast. In America, during the first decade, when production moved from the Atlantic coast (in particular New York and neighbouring New

---

39 Méliès' processing was done in an annex of the Theater Robert-Hudin, while colouring was entrusted to an external laboratory, run by Madame Elizabeth Thuillier, which continued to operate until the mid-30s.

40 Aldo Bernardini *Cinema muto italiano. Industria e organizzazione dello spettacolo*, 1905–1909, Editori Laterza 1981, p. 120: Bernardini, points out that this type of organisation arrived in Italy from abroad and was, therefore, more or less the same all over the world.

Jersey, but also in other places such as Florida or Chicago), to the Pacific and especially the drier climate of Los Angeles, several companies worked on wooden platforms covered at best just with diffuser sheets. Several films would be shot at the same time side by side, this certainly happened in Europe too, especially in France, at Pathé, which remained one of the largest – if not the largest – film producer during the first three decades of the film industry. When the need for greater realism arose, in America – but also elsewhere when filming large environments: dance halls, theatres ... – they often risked building complete *interiors* outdoors, sometimes with amusing effects of gusts of wind that scattered playing cards, blew out candles, made curtains fly or ruffled hair. Examples of these somewhat unusual images can be found even as late as 1915, in *The Birth of a Nation* by David W. Griffith, despite its relative advancement in structure and production. It is an extreme case, as it is extraordinary to see how Billy Bitzer (perhaps the first creative "author" of photography) was able to plan in those interiors *en pleine air* so as to get certain scenes of psychological significance from nature (i.e. the position of the sun), even using *backlighting*,[41] which notoriously cut the actor against the scene (the light on his hair!) increasing the three-dimensional effect. Working *on location*, an external set chosen for its appropriateness to the story in *The Birth of a Nation*, Bitzer also used a small white cloth to dampen the intensity of the sun, but only in close up, removing excessive contrast from the actors' faces (the scene where the Little Colonel's sister commits suicide after being chased by the black man Gus). These cloths, which are usually white but sometimes black (called "rags" in local jargon), are used to diffuse light or else partially or totally block it out and they still play an important role in the basic equipment of any lighting department.[42] We have taken a leap forward in time with these scenes from one of the fundamental films in the history of cinema. We need to fill in the details which led on from those first primitive film sets

41 *Backlight*, one of the *key* classical cinema lighting effects, became common practice with the advent of artificial lighting.

42 A basic multifunctional piece of equipment like everything in the world of cinema, "cloths" are used for light, but also as protection from rain (they can be dried by using lights of varying intensity), they can become improvised seats in uncomfortable exteriors and any other necessity that catches the imagination of practical people.

and allowed Griffith and Bitzer to foreshadow truly mature cinema, even formally.

Once the division of labour in these stable and multifunctional structures had been established in a continuous and complete cycle, the need for *reality* gradually took over, i.e. the fundamental element that distinguishes cinema from theatre, its older brother. While theatre bases its suggestion on allusion (especially when it reproduces natural environments), cinema needs to be closer to the truth it proposes. Thus, if at the outset every set was "painted", whether interior or landscape, a radical turning point came when reconstructed environments begin to alternate (as we continue to do today) with real exteriors. But at this point, historically, we cannot but underline the conflict between intuition and awareness. Because if attention had been paid to what was going on in England at that time, many steps forward would have been consciously taken straight away. Indeed, in that country fiction "interpreted" reality from the outset, perhaps with the idea of "recreating news" so that the public could participate in events generated by nature (eruptions) or by man (wars), which occurred in far away lands and could only be read in the newspapers up until then (by those who could read, of course). In *Attack on a China Mission*, made between 1900 and 1901, the Englishman James Williamson, chemist, pharmacist, photographer, and ultimately filmmaker, passed from actual news "alla Lumière" to "recreated" news. The camera holds a fixed long shot. The location "could" be the garden of an English style house in China, complete with a bay window. The action unravels (it seems that what has been preserved is incomplete) between the disruption of the missionary family's tranquility, the attack of the Chinese Boxers (with typical moustaches and tails) and the arrival of "reinforcements" (a platoon of sailors) that repel the attack. The rhythm, punctuated by entrances and the interaction of characters and masses, in its reconstruction of a "compressed" possible reality filmed without interruption, prefigures the necessity (as Georges Sadoul rightly observed)[43] for "dramaturgy". In reality, the exterior was William-

---

43 Georges Sadoul, *Storia generale del cinema. Le origini e i pionieri (1832–1909)*, Einaudi, Turin 1965, p. 415.

son's home (Ivy Lodge in Brighton) and several of his family (including his children) were among the many performers, at best dressed up rather than made up. Here then, fiction is applied to reality, using it with small but effective transformations. And just as we have seen that stopping the camera and resuming shortly afterwards escapes the viewer's perception of a different time other than "reality", likewise, except for a few friends, who would recognise the producer-director's home instead of the "missionary's residence in China"?

But, in England, the insights continued. We have already mentioned cinema's dependence on theatre and it seems appropriate at least to mention another possible relationship: with illustration. Towards the end of the century, illustration was developing through rather popular specialised magazines (satire, entertainment, youth, etc.) and becoming a regular feature in newspapers, giving birth, precisely in 1895, to the era of the "comic strip". It is storytelling that interests us, without words and without those sometimes rhyming texts at the foot of the images, as was used for subsequent strips. For example, in the magazine *Le Petit Français Illustré* on August 3, 1889, a strip was published in a series of six sketches *Historie sans paroles – Un Arroseur Public.*[44] A similar story had been drawn – this time only in 4 sketches – in 1893 for the calendar of the German newspaper *Fliegende Blatter.*[45] It is easy to guess that this is the gag of a gardener who is the victim of a practical joke: a boy who first turns off the water in a hose and then turns it on again. What we have here is something that might well have inspired what is considered the first fiction film, *Arroseur et Arrosé*, filmed by the Lumière brothers (and preserved) in three different versions between 1895 and 1897.

To return to England 1899, by intuition or by analogy with a comic strip, George Albert Smith pasted a scene between two *panoramic views*[46] by Cecil Hepworth, *View from an Engine Front* and *Train Leaving Tunnel*: in a railway carriage two newly-weds

44 Cited and reproduced by Donald Crafton in *Before Mickey. The Animated Film* 1898–1925, The MIT Press, Cambridge-London 1892.

45 Cited and reproduced by Attilio Giovannini in *Guida alla pubblicita' cinematografica*, Editrice dell'Ufficio Moderno, Milan 1957.

46 *A view* that was given the name *phantom ride* in England, highlighting the idea of *subjective*.

exchange affections, taking advantage of the darkness – which of course is not dark, otherwise how could we see anything? Among other things, this *The Kiss in the Tunnel* probably marks the conceptualisation of darkness, alongside cinematographic "night", which necessarily needs to show us what is happening (except for exceptional later cases where sound alone is used). It is difficult, if not impossible, to demonstrate whether the typical rhythm of the comic strip provided the sequencing here. Even if, for example, Edwin S. Porter, between 1903 and 1904, used human actors to cite the actual comic strip of the adventures of *Buster Brown* the enfant terrible created by Richard Felton Outcault[47] (animation was to be "rediscovered" a little later). To return to Smith, we are still in the field of genial intuitions because in addition to foreshadowing the idea of contrast montage *The Kiss in the Tunnel* is one of the first blends of real shots and reconstructed interiors. An intuition that Williamson was to take up again in 1901, in his famous *Fire!* finally producing a logical sequence of shots, and a first timid attempt at narrative *continuity*: a realistic first image of a *bobby* who realises that smoke is billowing from a house is followed by a shot with the orderly departure of some fire engines, probably a real life take of their race into the city, the arrival at the initial *location* (shot from exactly the same position) and the fire-fighters' work rendered dramatically realistic by a reconstructed interior with an asphyxiating man who is saved and carried down a ladder by a fireman. The element that provides the fluid external-internal-external *continuity* is the fireman in a montage that was to inspire Edwin S. Porter in his *The Life of an American Fireman*(1903).[48] A few years later, in 1905, Cecil Hepworth, the other great English pioneer, truly mastered *continuity* producing and acting with his wife, children and dog in *Rescued by Rover* (directed by Lewin Fitzhamon) – Rover of course was the dog.

47 Among other things, R. F. Outcault (1863–1928) was also the author of *Yellow Kid* the first comic strip character ever, Sunday 7 July, 1895, in a colour supplement attached to the "New York World" published by Pulitzer.

48 Porter makes matters much more complex by having the firemen enter the burning house several times where not a man but a woman, and a mother to boot, is in danger. But, initially (and the *paperprint* of the *copyright* confirms it), Williamson operated a single interior insert showing the actions in succession first inside, then outside. Only a few years later did he, or someone else, cross-cut the two parts, finally giving the viewer perfect continuity of action in the internal-external sequence.

Interiors and exteriors effectively alternate because (and this is the true meaning of *continuity*, even today), each shot makes up an integral whole which, through the character's comings and goings, conveys the logic that leads to solving a mystery and a *happy end* (the smart dog who finds the kidnapped child and then retraces the path with its owner). For its time, the film was a huge success and copies were ordered from all over the world. This caused progressive damage to the original negative, which had to be reassembled, from time to time, using *doubles*[49] of scenes that had initially been discarded. It seems that *Rescued by Rover* is one of the first surviving examples of a film that required several shots of the same scene, especially because of the dog's obviously autonomous behaviour (as can be noted in some second generation copies.[50] Restoring and studying the various versions, Harold Brown, the first head of film conservation of the BFI, realised that to obtain the correct succession of various shots, tiny holes had been made in progressive number on the various selected negative segments. At that time, and for many years to come (the moviola was a much later invention), montage meant identifying the points where to cut using a magnifying glass, then scraping part of the emulsion equivalent to the space between two perforations (one on the right and one on the left, about a quarter of the useful surface between the frames) and gluing it to another piece using a mixture of acetone in which pieces of nitrocellulose film were dissolved. We shall see that this operation became extremely complicated with the advent of colour film.

To return to external-internal alternation, we could hardly say that the painted sets used by Hepworth were extraordinary. If the truth be told, the reconstructions built almost anywhere were still theatrical in style and in many cases even the exteriors were simulated. The largest film studio during these first fifteen years of cinema was the Gaumont in Buttes-Chaumont (45m by 20m

---

49   According to another hypothesis, the film was shot again in its entirety several times, scene by scene.

50   In copies from Argentina, in one of the replaced shots, following the dog that is forced to swim across a small river (despite the fact that its owner uses a boat), the camera moves to the right and reveals ... a bridge: the obedient dog, however intelligent, could not understand why he had to swim when both a boat and a bridge were available.

and 34m high); the Pathé studio in Montreuil-sous-Bois (a stone's throw away from Méliès' studio), was continuously enlarged and enhanced between 1904 and 1907, it became quite impressive and even had a small pool with running water. Such efforts may appear (affectionately) ridiculous from today's point of view. In a scene from *Au bagne* (Ferdinand Zecca, 1905) for example, a long "obvious" lateral tracking shot follows a group of prisoners loading and unloading on a dock, a very large painted backdrop shows the sky and ships in the background. The trolley stops when a full scale side of a ship appears on the left. In no way does the painted background manage to merge with the rippling stream of water just below the gangway. Water also appears in the view from the deck of a battleship, with an officer seen from behind firing cannons towards a miniature reconstructed Odessa. Through a telescope he checks the effect of his shots on the model city on the other side of the water and sees realistic agitated and wounded people. The scene is form the first rendition of the Battleship Potëmkin *La Révolution en Russie* by Lucien Nonguet, filmed in 1905, therefore a reconstructed version of those news events. Earlier, though still in 1905, Nonguet had described another war, the Russian-Japanese war (*Événements russo-japonais*), in sixteen short chapters. And while during some outdoor scenes he reached the point of canceling some too obviously French lettering from a train, scratching them with a blunt[51] instrument, a painted bird's eye view of Port-Arthur is overshadowed by its attackers, cannons and the fumes of explosions!!!. But one of the most striking cases of the nonchalant way in which "profilmic material" was used at the time concerns Edwin S. Porter. It seems as if light years instead of just four months (at least according to the copyright – from the end of June to the beginning of December 1903) separate *Uncle Tom's Cabin* from *The Great Train Robbery*. In the former, an excessively condensed version of Beecher Stowe's novel, theatrical "clichés" abound, even a rolling painted canvas simulating

---

51 Scratches deliberately made on the gelatine or substrate can be found quite frequently. Not having the originals it is difficult to tell whether they were engraved copy by copy of directly on the negative. The latter case could concern the need to remove *copyright* symbols (as can be seen for example in an English copy of *The Trip to the Moon*, by Méliès which was probably pirated). While marks to simulate wind in a storm were surely applied to the negative of *Odissea* by Bertolini and Pavan, produced by Milano Film in 1911.

a flowing river of ice. Instead of being filmed in sequence against different backgrounds, an identical shot of a dog running right to left on the banks of the river is simply repeated three times creating an incredibly estranging effect; not to mention the cotton fields that fail to render any depth whatsoever in their graphic representation. And after that, instead, the miracle of *The Great Train Robbery*, with a precise quest for realism by means of technical effects. A matte is used to mask portions of the scene allowing for the insertion, in the first scene, of a train arriving (visible through the window of the ticket office), and in the third, a landscape flowing past (seen through the open door of the mail car). The quality is even more obvious if you compare it with a plagiarised version shot by Lubin seven months later (27 June, 1904), where the ticket office set was built under the blazing sun right next to a real little railway station, and a rotating drum with bushes and trees painted on it is blatantly used to simulate the train's movement seen through an open door inside a painted wagon (the idea of this large cylinder which provided *relative motion* compared to the static camera belongs, as usual, to Méliès).[52]

We are, of course, jumping ahead and describing not so much the actual "first times" of some expedient or grammatical element (which in some cases can no longer be directly verified since the works in question have been lost), but examples which can, as far as possible, be demonstrated with relative ease using what is available today (video-DVD, etc.). As long as the narrative proceeded scene by scene in one single shot, it would take years to reach a truly persuasive stage space from a grammatical point of view. It was necessary to pass through intermediate stages. In *Ben Hur* by Sidney Olcott and Frank O. Rose (by Kalem Studios, 1907) we have a paradox. To convey the splendour of ancient Rome, they built (or perhaps they borrowed from a theatre, like the costumes) several backdrops, but since the chariot race in the final scene called for a very large spaces to show the vehicles better, three or

---

52 Rotating cylinders, but also rotating three-dimensional miniatures so as to create the effect of a *panned* landscapes that would otherwise have been impossible to film: something akin to the saying about Muhammad and the mountain. The principle is simple: while the camera, if desired, can move, the projector, of course, remains fixed. So, for relative motion, either the camera is set on self-propelled supports while actually filming (dolly, etc.) or motion is recreated in front of a fixed camera by moving the background.

four of these large rectangular canvases, showing temple paintings, flights of steps and so on, were lined up side by side, diagonally instead of facing the camera, thus destroying any possibility of perspective through the obvious flatness of these items of scenery. In Italy, however, particular attention was being paid to perspective, and not only elevating the point of view of the camera but also tilting the floor of the studio, as is normal in a theatre. This way it was possible to create accomplished perspective effects using flats, which created fascinating visual effects akin to the Palladian Teatro Olimpico in Vicenza. One of the most successful examples of this is *Nerone* by Maggi and Ambrosio, produced by Ambrosio in 1909. A decisive step, and perhaps not only regarding Italy, was taken by Giovanni Pastrone. With the complicity of set designer Luigi Borgogno, Pastrone created large classical colonnades with an off-centre vanishing point on the one hand (as had already been done in *Nerone*) but, on the other, he finally built a completely three-dimensional reproduction of the exterior of the city wall. Besides being the first *two reel film* produced in Italy (March 1911), *The Fall of Troy* marked a point of no return in set design. Though the walls still appeared smooth, because the boulders were only painted, and the famous horse was just a cutout, the dimensions were beginning to be more impressive and, moreover, the scenes were populated by hundreds of correctly dressed extras (in helmets with armour and shields) who act in a suitably agitated manner. Eventually these qualities would be deemed defects, but only after the release of *Cabiria* (April 1914) where the reality of the scenery was perfected (the papier-mâché now reproduced the physical features of city walls, temples, houses and palaces, both indoors and outdoors) to the point that the camera had no choice but to move within it.

Chapter Nine

Camera movements

To return to our definition, *Cabiria* was the first film with conscious camera movements which became necessary to enhance the three-dimensional film set that had been created. This is not to say that the camera had been strictly immobile before this. Considering the grandeur of the Pathé studio, we have already mentioned a tracking shot in *Au bagne*, and there had been others in several productions. These can be defined as "obvious" because they reiterated movement, following the dynamics of the action. The first platforms supporting equipment for "animated photography" needed to be "extremely solid, because, the slightest movement had to be avoided at all costs, otherwise the images would be unstable and the background would jump on the screen",[53] Tripods were recommended, in particular the sturdiest ones, and mechanisms were gradually added that were activated turning a crank or handle. Among such accessories we find the *Panoramic platform* in the 1905 Pathé Frères Catalog: "This platform for panoramic shots consists of a base with a large toothed wheel controlled by a tangent screw that is operated by a crank [...]".[54]

But, in the precautions for use, we read:

> "We must warn our customers that to obtain good results using a panoramic platform requires some experience: we wish to point out that beginners have the tendency to pan too quickly, the resulting images are completely lacking in sharpness".[55]

Only in 1909 did a manual give a description of another important instrument: "the figure [...] shows a device that allows for the

---

53 E. Trutat, *La photographie animée* ... cit., p. 147.

54 *Anciens Etablissements Pathé Frères, Appareils & Accessoires*, April 1905, p. 67.

55 Ibid, p. 67.

inclination of the camera, in order to direct it towards the subject, as it approaches; this is also moved by turning a crank".[56] It was a device that could be mounted above what had already been named a *rotating head* which therefore allowed vertical, in today's terminology, in addition to horizontal panning. It is interesting to note how the use of this device was described at the time. *Panoramic view* is understood as descriptive and not as *the camera following* movements and actions, and "a device that allows for the inclination of the camera, in order to be able to direct it towards the subject", as if to reproach Georges Méliès who, to obtain a sight enlargement or reduction of a subject,[57] built an inclined plane to keep the subject constantly centred, since he noted that approaching or moving away from the camera caused a natural variation of axis; he never thought of moving the camera. In this case though, more than moving the camera to follow the action, the main emphasis is on its logical function. Yet, even before the aforementioned publications "obvious" panoramic shots could be found, even combined shots (horizontal plus vertical, although at that point it was necessary to turn three cranks, the one that ran the actual camera obviously being the fundamental one): the extraordinary (right–left) shot, for example, that follows the arrival of the fire brigade on its way to the burning house with the woman at the window in *The Life of an American Fireman* and then two such shots in *The Great Train Robbery* (both dated 1903). The first (left-right) accompanies the bandits hiding behind the water tank as they sneak aboard the train. The second, when, after robbing the passengers and taking off with just the locomotive (switching track – an obvious error of *continuity*), they stop to continue on foot and here from horizontal, following the rascals' descent from the elevated tracks the shot moves vertically downwards. This is the meaning of "obvious": the characters move and we cannot but follow them. This was the case in the Pathé studios

---

56 F. Paul Liesegang, *Il cinematografo. Manuale di cinematografia*, Fratelli Bocca Editori, Milan-Rome, 1909, p. 350.

57 This very complex technique was thought to have been used for the first time in 1902 for Méliès' famous *L'homme à la tête en caoutchouc*. However, in 1999 Lobster Films in Paris discovered no less than 17 films by Méliès that were considered lost, showing the use of this expedient at least a year earlier as it is found both in *Le diable géant* ou *Le miracle de la madone* and in *Nain et géant* both made in 1901.

described above which was equipped with a track for sliding the camera but only in accordance with the amount of background needed in a shot, indeed many primitive studios used one (perhaps this was also the initial idea in Montreuil).

In *Cabiria*, on the other hand, the movement was always conceived and then executed primarily to give added value to what was being represented: a linguistic element therefore that was no longer just "obvious" but "aware".

> Using this system the camera could be moved gradually, over a considerable space, always consciously following the logic of the scene, capturing its development and showing a succession of objects from different perspectives. This conveyed a sufficiently strong three dimensional impression to the audience which would last afterwards even when other parts of the scene were filmed form a static point of view. This is due to the ease with which the human eye grasps and preserves an impression of depth once it has been established.[58]

This reasoning, presented in the patent application that formalised the use of the *dolly* in cinema, is of considerable significance especially psychologically. And if "it consisted of a tripod where the steel points, which guaranteed stability, were replaced by ball bearings that allowed movement [...] this was also done by the director using Decauville rails"[59] this moment marked not only the beginning the era of real three-dimensionality, but also that of deeper meaning. Not only because the camera began to do that which we are not allowed to do (to approach our interlocutor, peer into their eyes or dwell in a detail of their clothing...), but because it went beyond the lifelikeness of photography, taking on psychological values that are, however complex, simply, intuitively and universally understood.

Nevertheless, like many of his fellow early directors, at least once in his progressive epic, whether consciously or unconsciously, Pastrone still feared that his viewers would not fully understand him. So when, at the beginning of the film, the survivors, having escaped the eruption – as D'Annunzio writes – "divide the booty"

---

58 From the patent, in French, dated 17 February, 1913, appearing in photograph in Giovanni Pastrone *Cabiria*, National Cinema Museum, Turin, 1977, p. 15.

59 Maria Adriana Prolo, in the introduction to the volume above, p. 15.

stolen from the villa's cellar (and the camera pans to a group on the left where the little Cabiria sits with the nurse Croessa), among the jewels is a ring with a cameo which the nurse immediately appropriates. To make us understand the decisive importance this ring will have later in the story, Pastrone makes a direct cut and gives us a detail: Croessa's hands holding the ring. But the background to this detail is not the meadow where the group is sitting, but a dark cloth. An enlarged shot detached from the camera's usual movement as if the spectator were otherwise be unable to "decontextualise" the ring. In the next development of language and until the end of the silent era, irises and mattes of every shape, obscuring the contours of images to a greater or lesser extent, would indicate where the eye should be directed; even to the point of *widening* or *tightening* the space for an object or scene, almost anticipating the zoom. But before the introduction of this repertoire of rhetorical devices, close-ups and details, especially when they highlighted or cut to details from a whole scene, tended to be justified in an excessive manner or even decontextualised as Pastrone did in *Cabiria*.

Plate 1

Top: A projection using Reynaud's Théâtre optique reconstructed at the Grévin Museum.
Centre: The Lumière Cinematograph as a projector (right) and camera (left).
Bottom: Original negative and positive frames.

Plate 2

Top: Méliès' studio in Montreuil.
Centre: Work inside the studio.
Bottom: An original frame from *L'homme mouche*
(*The Human Fly*, Méliès, 1902).

Plate 3

Top: Cinema pavilion in 1898.
Centre: Indoor scene shot outdoors.
Bottom: A frame from *Bassin des Tuileries*
(L. Lumière, 1896).

Plate 4

Top: Work in progress at studio Pathé in
Montreuil (1904).
Centre: A scene being shot outdoors.
Bottom: A tinted frame from the *Fall of Troy*
(G. Pastrone and R. L. Borgnetto, 1911).

Plate 5

Top: Shooting a scene at the Messter studio (1906).
Centre from left to right:
Two Kinemacolor frames (1906); the frames
superimposed showing the additive effect of
Kinemacolor and Chronochrome; three
Chronochrome frames (1912).
Bottom: A stencil coloured frame from a
phonoscène.

Plate 6

Top: Griffith directing *Way Down East* (1920)
outdoors with reinforced artificial lighting.
Centre: Building the set for Ernst Lubitsch's
Anna Boleyn (1920).
Bottom: A tinted Pathé frame with the company
name printed on the side.

Plate 7

Top: Henry King directs *Romola* (1925): a
three-dimensional film set in the background.
Bottom: Split Screen effect in Alberto Cavalcanti's
Nothing But Time (1926).

Plate 8

Top: Shooting Lloyd Bacon's *Cain and Mabel* (1936)
at the Warner Studios.
Bottom: A tinted and toned frame: sunset effect.

Plate 9

Top: Live sound recording for a documentary by
Francesco Pasinetti, Venice (1942).
Centre: Vittorio De Sica behind the camera on the
set of *Bicycle Thieves* (1948).
Bottom: A frame with a variable density soundtrack.

Plate 10

Top: A reconstruction of a ship at the Columbia
studios: *Hell Below Zero* (1954) by Mark Robson.
Centre: Setting up the lights for a take in Mario
Costa's *Revelation* (1955).
Bottom: A frame with a variable area soundtrack.

Plate 11

Top: Filming in VistaVision: *The Errand Boy* (1961)
by and starring Jerry Lewis.
Centre: Truffaut filming on the streets during
the 60s.
Bottom: A Technicolor Tripack frame.

Plate 12

Top: Filming Gene Kelly's *Hello, Dolly* (1969) at the Fox studios.
Centre: George Lucas setting up special effects in *Star Wars* (1977).
Bottom: A CinemaScope frame with a magnetic sound track and deteriorated colours.

Plate 13

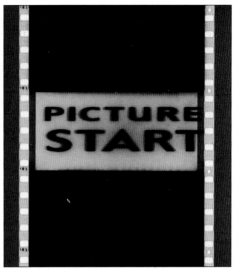

From the top: Positive and negative Lumière 70mm frames; a 70mm frame with a magnetic sound track; a horizontal IMAX 70mm frame; a Widescreen negative frame;

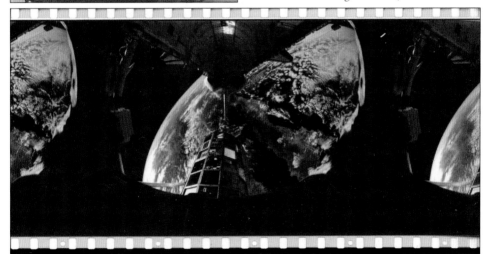

Plate 14

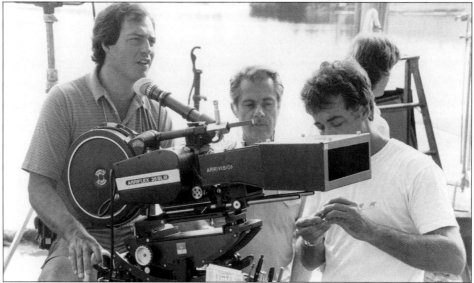

Top: During the filming of Steven Spielberg's
Jaws (1975): one of the animatronics.
Centre: The 3D camera used for Joe Alves's *Jaws
3-D* (1983).
Bottom: A pair of three-dimensional frames from
Jaws 3-D.

Plate 15

Top: The body-mount camera, a system similar
to the Steadicam.
Centre: Vittorio Storaro testing HDTV in Venice
(*Arlecchino*, 1983, by Giuliano Montaldo).
Bottom: A positive widescreen frame.

Plate 16

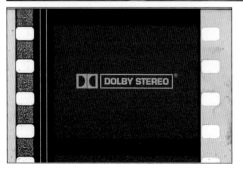

Top: The pre-digital film *Who Framed Roger Rabbit*
(1988) by Robert Zemeckis.
Centre: Green screens, for subsequent
compositing, used at St. Marks' in Lasse
Hallström's *Casanova* (2005).
Bottom: An original Dolby frame with the digital
code set between the perforations.

Chapter Ten

Close-ups, details

ere we need to turn back and take it again from England. In 1900 Albert Smith's *Grandma's Reading Glass* introduced *detail,* in other words an enlargement focused on a person or object within a larger image, which then becomes a sort of *leitmotiv* in this little film. And it is done in a "logical" manner, not only by using circular vignetting to indicate the actual object used for enlargement, but the object itself is absolutely obvious within the dynamics of the story: a large magnifying glass used by a boy to look at various things while playing with his grandmother e.g. his grandmother's eye, a kitten. The matte that blacks out the rest of the image makes the round lens patently clear and therefore justifies the use of detail, most important of all it makes a necessary logical break between the overall scene, which returns periodically, and the various details. Over the following years the pursuit of this logic led to an effusion of spyglasses, telescopes and even keyholes or whatever else could justify closeups, often with delightfully mischievous intent. Méliès, as usual, pushed it further and transformed the detail of an eye into face of the moon (*Au clair de la lune,* 1903) watching over a typical, resigned, poetically persecuted Pierrot: but in this case (using matte and counter-matte) the detail is set surreally into more complex whole. Nonetheless, *detail* and *close-up* acquired a real narrative and linguistic function once it was no longer considered necessary to justify their use. As occurred, still in 1903 and still in England, and thanks again to Smith, first in *Sick Kitten* where two children play with a kitten and the little girl feeds it (in an *extreme close-up*); and then in the delightful *Mary Jane's Mishap* which actually begins with a close-up of a serving girl working in the kitchen. The close-up returns several times alternating with a long shot of the kitchen, recounting first the mess she makes with shoe polish, getting it all over her face, and then with paraffin when she sets herself on fire and quite comically dispatching herself to the next world. This, however, affords her the opportunity to terrify her friends by rising as a spirit from her grave (an ironic anticipation of certain De Palma finales) ... On the other hand, in *Vie et Passion de NS Jésus Christ* dated 1907, Ferdinand Zecca, presents close-ups for both *ecce homo* and *the miracle de St. Veronica*. His complete cuts almost prefigure Pastrone's scrupulous use of a neutral backgrounds, first for the close-up of Christ beaten and crowned with thorns (he even employs an explanatory script), and then for Veronica holding the veil bearing the image of the bleeding face of Christ. Rather than a technical strategy however, in this case the images seems more like a need to evoke popular holy prints (prayer cards) which pervade the aesthetic style of the entire film. But it was surely strategy that informed Pastrone, for fear that that ring, which would no longer be shown close up, might not register with the viewer when later flaunted and recognised by the characters, triggering further developments in the plot.

In those years, while the grammar of cinema was being moulded between instinct and awareness, other formal "anomalies" can be found sometimes connected to the succession of frames of different widths. Indeed, when *axial cuts* began to be employed (jumping in from a long or medium shot to a close-up, or vice versa), and fluid movement needed to be preserved across those different cuts, the movement was replicated instead of being assembled coherently. In Porter's small masterpiece *Dream of a Rarebit Fiend* (1906), based on Winsor McCay's comic strips, during a nightmare the greedy consumer of heavy toasted cheese slices falls from his flying bed and ends up caught by the tail of his nightshirt on the weathervane of a bell tower. The long shot (a painted background and with a cardboard silhouette of the falling actor – probably filmed *frame-by-frame*,[60]) follows a close up where a piece of torn nightshirt remained dangling after our poor man had already fallen from sight. But we find him back in place in the long shot and the fall is repeated in its entirety. Was it fear that the action

---

60 Frame by frame, means *one turn one picture*: different ways of calling the (sublimation of substitution) technique that allows for the animation of drawings, cardboard cutouts, various objects, various materials, human beings, and so on.

was too fast and would be missed? Or was it a misunderstanding of cinematographic *time*? In any case, it is precisely in the sequencing of times that anomalies are still found in these early examples of chronological narrative. Starting, at least, from *The Life of an American Fireman*: the firefighters are suddenly woken in their dormitory above the engine house, they rush to the classic pole and slide down to their ever-ready fire trucks: but it actually takes so long for them to slide down that it seems they came not from the floor above but from the fiftieth floor! And while Porter's film is from 1903, Méliès replicated the same imperfection several years later, in 1907, showing another fall (an old astronomer leans too far out from his balcony and ends up falling into a barrel of water) resulting in an equally interminable descent: *Eclipse de soleil en pleine lune*.

Chapter Eleven

Towards a grammar and a syntax of narrative

So, now we can define, broadly speaking, the long, difficult, endless research that, over almost twenty years, laid the foundations of film grammar: the set of technological discoveries which became the terminology and rules that were to make the narrative and expressive complexity of the new audio-visual language possible (sometimes linguistic development can be the catalyst of technology, but much more often the opposite occurs).

And we also say audio of course, given that sound had never been abandoned since Edison's initial research and it proved decisive in establishing the technological basis of "animated photography". Throughout the prehistory and the whole proto-history of cinema the technological quest to couple images with music and speech continued, with poor results; it was live music that became the complement to each projection. It was initially justified by the idea of equating cinema to theatrical "pantomime" (mime + dance + music, in all possible variations) and, we should remember moreover, that music also accompanied Emile Reynaud's spectacles. Likewise, dance interludes were frequently inserted during projections in the first fifteen years. This theater-cinema parallel often conditioned the expressive manner of those early years (with main characters approaching the camera as if it were the proscenium, and sometimes winking at the audience, every gesture was frontal and turning one's back on the camera was strictly prohibited), indeed, even to the point of using a full live orchestra. But what really delayed the birth of sound cinema tout-court was the technical inability to ensure reliable synchronisation between sound and image, and above all, the shortcomings in the amplification of phonographic cylinders first and subsequently of gramophone discs. We will discuss this later.

The threshold of this long and complex narrative that we have already in some ways hinted at in *Cabiria* and *Birth of a Nation*, was marked by other important steps forward. Projection quality was becoming ever more reliable thanks to the almost exclusive use of arc lamps, and therefore electricity. The spaces used for projection were also improving, from small restructured ground floors (warehouses, shops) or small reconverted theatres (cine-variety shows continued to function for many years) to real theatres designed exclusively for film projections. The Gaumont Palace in Paris, inaugurated on 11 October, 1911, was for a long time the "largest cinema in the world" with a capacity of 3,400. And then there was the standardisation of film stock, approved at Congrès International des Fabricants de Film in February 1909, chaired by Georges Méliès and attended by major figures of the expanding industry, including George Eastman. The decision made was to universally adopt the perforations (four per frame on both sides of 35mm film) as anticipated by Edison and subsequently homogenised by the American manufacturer Bell and Howell.[61] With some slight adjustments, these are the perforations still in use in negative film today. A slight curvature in the vertical contours allows for great stability in the passage of the film through the mechanical parts (first of all, the *claw*). However, in the systematic and continuous use of positive prints for projection, it was a design that developed cracks over time between the curved and the straight horizontal part of the perforation and inevitably led to frequent breakages. So, in 1924 Kodak introduced a new type of rectangular perforation for prints (compatible with the previous ones) but with the corners slightly rounded and this remains the standard across the world (except in the Eastern block where it was only adopted after the fall of the iron curtain). This standard, which obliged manufacturers of equipment (cameras,

---

61 Founded in Chicago in 1907 by projectionist Donald H. Bell and repair mechanic Albert S. Howell, Bell and Howell designed and built the most reliable cameras, projectors and accessories. In 1908 they commercialised a perforating machine which soon established itself as superior to others, thus spreading that specific type of *hole* first in the United States and then in the rest of the world.

projectors, etc.) and film stock all over the world to adopt uniform specifications, allowed not only for universal exchange of films, but finally made rental a valid alternative to sale, the commercial practice until then.

However, *Cabiria* was not immediately rented out, nor was *Birth of a Nation* in its first months. Indeed, in both cases the *premiere* was managed directly by the respective producers, with the creation of unique and unrepeatable events. Griffith's film was programmed to open city after city, with cinematography making its official entry into theatres and opera houses rented for the occasion. Programmes were printed that finally listed at least the actors, if not all the production team, and musical scores, completely or partially composed *ex novo* were performed with orchestra, choir, soloists as well as sound effects. As the brain-child of poet, writer and playwright Gabriele D'Annunzio, the Italian *film*[62] had added intellectual and especially promotional value. Griffith's work, on the other hand, met with socio-political fallout in accusations of racism and violent public discussion, a controversy that still resonates today. And the echo that ensued, in both cases, even among the non-specialised press, ensured the definitive positioning of cinema among the artworks of human creativity and ingenuity manifested through a conscious and autonomous language.

A language which, in *Cabiria*, took full life-like command of the scenic space, with sumptuous reconstructions of palaces, city walls, temples, and perfectly furnished interiors. Reconstructed outdoors, both open air and in the film studio, for example the colonnades of the villa that collapse during the eruption – crushing some extras this time (collapsing columns also appeared at the end of *The Fall of Troy*, but it was planned to occur exactly when the actors had moved away ...); or on the roof of the temple of Moloch where Maciste throws one of the pursuers into a great steaming brazier. External reconstructions like the walls of Syracuse that should look out to sea, though there was no sea there despite a full scale Roman galley going up in flames (Archimedes' burning mirrors!), models of ships filmed separately (in double exposure)

---

62 Initially, in Italian the word *film* was used both for the material and the entertainment, the English word film was thus Italianised in the feminine to mean the countable noun.

were added thanks to the professional skill of Segundo de Chomón.[63] And then there were real *locations*, exteriors filmed in the Alps, with elephants from Africa, with the deserts and encampments destroyed (but not too much), achieved through an appropriate overlapping of images. Moreover, the confident and appropriate application of colours (through toning and dye transfer), was a precious and spectacular addition. And then there was that camera in continuous movement enhancing the set space and began to emphasis the action. There were rare, but highly intense cuts into close-ups that focus, during the "Sinfonia del Fuoco" scene, on details of hands praying or pushing the young sacrificial victim into the fiery belly of the bloodthirsty god (these deleted shots have only recently been rediscovered and reassembled). Of course, though not yet totally rhythmic, the montage was instrumental in this, and there is occasional sluggishness and some awkward moments where the dolly cannot be interrupted in its representation of real time. An analysis of discarded takes of the same scenes, however, made during the recent restoration, reveals the actual experimentation that was undertaken in many shots which were not so much repeated as filmed in different ways so as to choose the most effective one.[64]

On the other hand, Griffith, in *Birth of a Nation*, fully defined his personal style, which was very different from Pastrone's and essentially based on the use on ellipsis, therefore on cuts. He mounted sequences of very short shots that basically came to define the full range of the director' repertoire: from the long shot (battlefields, the besieged hut seen from above) to details (animals, the daguerreotype of Elsie Stoneman). Without using tracking except for a few very effective *camera car shots* (the assault on the enemy trenches, the ride of the Ku Klux Klan). Panning is used in an equally effective and essential way, to the point of

---

63 Catalonian technician Segundo de Chomón was extraordinary in his use of colourings and special photographic effects. He worked a lot for Pathé, in competition with Méliès, and was called to Italy by Giovanni Pastrone to work for Itala Film. He collaborated in *Cabiria* and, among others, created animations for *La guerra e il sogno di Momi* (1917). He ended his successful career alongside Abel Gance, inventing the special effects for the film *Napoleon* (1927).

64 See Paolo Bertetto and Gianni Rondolino (edited by) *Cabiria e il suo tempo*, Museo Nazionale del Cinema-Editrice Il Castoro 1998.

overcoming the objectivity of the images by conceptualising them (from a mother with her crying children on the ruins of their hut panning right over the huge valley and the army on the march). Like burning fires or better still the eruption in *Cabiria*, he used composite images of despairing extras and burning miniatures. Griffith preferred the *medium full shot* which he himself codified, by cutting the actor around the knees, it allowed the setting and the expression of body and face to be viewed at the same time. He worked on several actions contemporaneously that merged into one (Griffith's "parallel montage"). And while the ending with the gathering of the Klan and attack on the Black militia is spectacularly incisive and engaging, the most persuasive sequence is the attempted rape of the little Colonel's younger sister Flora, because it is pervaded by psychological nuance and effective sequencing of both time and frame. First, he reaffirms the innocence of the adolescent, as she reaches the well she in enchanted by nature, observing a squirrel on tree in detail; meanwhile the treacherous renegade Gus conveys his whole animal desire in an extreme close-up. The ensuing pursuit, with Flora's brother following behind with growing agitation, ends with her tragic final suicide to save her honour. Moreover, those self-contained and apparently disjointed shots which reinforce the narrative tension (the Cameron family reunited in pain), are the fruit of Griffith's experimentation in more than three hundred *one reel* and *two reels* films. We are referring, in particular, to a sudden cut in *The Lonely Villa* (1909). While thieves are breaking through the fragile defences put in place by a mother and her daughters in an isolated villa, the woman calls her husband, who had been artfully removed earlier, suddenly we see one of the bandits – framed from below – cutting the telephone cable. To underline the ensuing drama after that sudden shot, among other things, Griffith cuts in from the previous full shot, to a medium full shot for both the husband in the saloon and the woman in the room, reinforcing the effect of the interrupted phone call. Let us return, finally, to *Birth of a Nation*, and some little touches that begin, structurally, to make even backgrounds vital and realistic. For example, at the entrance of the temporary hospital in the Library of Congress where the Little Colonel lies wounded, while Elsie Stoneman accompanies mother Cameron, who has just taken leave of her son, she attracts the attention of a sighing guard who cannot take his eyes off her.

Finally, both these pivotal works made occasional use of artificial lighting, which was already quite mature, at least in the case of *Cabiria*, either reinforcing sunlight, or creating suggestive effects.

Let us return now to these various technological elements which, having overcome the long apprenticeship period described above, have allowed and continue to allow this language to develop in expressiveness.

Chapter Twelve

Silent Movies

Film

> Bands of film, or simply film, are the strips of photographs used in film screenings. They are varying lengths of celluloid strips – up to 300 meters and 35mm wide: the universal type. [...]. Each meter of film contains 54 images – each image being 23mm wide and 18mm high. Film strips have two sides, one smooth and shiny, the other opaque and slightly rough. The shiny one is natural while the opaque and slightly rough one is the side containing the gelatin. It is precisely on this latter that the photography exists. Film has equidistant holes on either side that fit the teeth of a rotating drum, if the projector apparatus is an Edison system, and forks (claws), if the device uses the Lumière system.[65]

The above description of the fundamental component of cinema, taken from the first reliable Italian manual (1907), may seem a little cryptic by today's standards. But the principles outlined remain constant, the measurements first of all. Film is still 35 mm wide, perforated on the sides, and contains 52 instead of 54 frames per meter. The size of the frame has changed over the years since the surface has been adapted (or obliged) to host more information.

The support, the "smooth and shiny" face described by Re, is celluloid, actually nitrocellulose – a compound also used for an explosive commonly called flash cotton – which becomes plastic by adding camphor. It was developed in 1869 by the American John Wesley Hyatt and can be considered the first modern organic plastic material (i.e. not derived from chemical synthesis). Used initially to make billiard balls, as a propellant, for making cuffs for ceremonial clothing and some other everyday items (combs,

---

65   G. Re, *Il cinematografo* ..., cit., p. 55.

toys, etc.), celluloid was adapted to the budding photographic industry first by John C. Carbutt and then by George Eastman (assisted in his research by Harry Reichembach), both in 1889. This gave rise to endless legal disputes between the Eastman Dry Plate and Film Company and Ansco, a factory that had acquired Carbutt's patent (the Eastman Kodak Company was not established until May 1892). As already mentioned, Eastman provided Dickson with the first ¾ inch (19mm) emulsified celluloid strips, perforated only on one side, that fed horizontally through the camera and, much like photographs for initial mass consumption, produced images with rounded *vignetting*. There were only 7 experiments, all dated 1891, surviving fragments include a child playing with clubs in *Indian Club Swinger*.[66] In 1892, with commercialisation in mind, an improved apparatus employed a wider strip, perforated on both sides (at first 1½ inches and then, 1 inch 9/16 roughly, the fateful 35mm),[67] with vertical movement. Each length of film was 50 feet (about 17m). The light-sensitive emulsion, however, was not made by Kodak but by the Blair Camera Company, which had also started producing film in 1891, leading to endless, quarrelsome competition with the Eastman company. The decision was motivated both by real problems that Kodak was experiencing in the manufacture of material and, above all, by the *frosted* appearance of the Blair product which made it more suitable for use in the Kinetoscope – with uniform illumination from a pointed light source – but, the same factor made it inadequate for projection. Both Edison and later the Lumière brothers, in an attempt to make the most of the surface, adopted a ratio between height and width of 4:3 (actually about 24 and not 23 mm, by 18) which remained unchanged during the whole silent era – translated in reverse it is 1: 1.33, the proportion used in technical descriptions. The line separating one frame and another was minimal, almost non-existent. The *window* (or *matte*) that controlled light input in the film camera was always slightly larger

66 See Charles Musser, *Edison Motion Pictures, 1890–1900, An Annotated Filmography*, Le Giornate del Cinema Muto, Smithsonian Institution Press, 1997, p. 73 and ff.

67 "35mm film was initially made by splitting 70mm (2 3/4") Eastman film for photo cameras in two." Harold Brown and Kevin Patton, *Come trattare le vecchie pellicole*, "Griffithiana" 29/30, September 1987, p. 70.

than its counterpart in the projector, where the light source returns the image to the screen, so that the extreme limits were not obvious, they could vary depending on the type of camera used. Indeed, according to some period publications it was possible to recognise the specific standards of a given manufacturer by the way the frames were positioned in relation to the perforations.[68] As already mentioned, Edison initially used four rectangular perforations on both sides of the film, while the Lumière brothers had a single round one. However, at the Paris Congress in 1909, after a failed attempt the previous year, a definitive standard for perforations was sought; up until 1905 anarchy had reigned. Initially, film stock had been produced without perforations and manufacturer-producers, who built both cameras and projectors and also made films, could invent their own standard that were totally incompatible with others. Thus, in the early years perforations had to be made by hand and in total darkness. Later this operation was entrusted to machines which could not afford to make mistakes, especially with negatives as even a slight error in "pitch" (the distance between two successive perforations) meant the destruction of the film and therefore the footage in question.

A unique case was the system developed by the American Biograph to get around Edison's *copyright* where perforation was carried out at the same time as filming. Using a broad 68mm format, the company's initial idea was to produce images printed on photographic paper for their device (the Mutoscope), an individual viewing device that was to replace the Kinetoscope, thanks to its facility of use.[69] But it was not Biograph that first introduced the *wide format*. Continuing his research into movement analysis, Étienne-Jules Marey, had also adopted a 90mm format (without perforations) when he perfected his *chronophotography* in 1890

68 In the one issue of Sonzogno's *Enciclopedia Figurata* dedicated to cinema, dated June 1928, Gaumont is defined as having a frame line set exactly in the middle of a perforation while Pathé's instead was halfway between two holes. In truth, descriptions of such features in earlier manuals are vague. This different location of images led to the problem of *misframing* which we will tackle when we deal with projectors.

69 The Mutoscope remained in use for a long time, though the company also started to project the same films, which had extraordinary definition if we consider the format, for normal production and distribution at 35mm.

and changed from sensitised paper to celluloid. His assistant Georges Demenÿ, in turn, used 60mm unperforated film, when he set up his own business developing at least three patents (1892–1895) that failed to establish themselves on the market despite his partnership with the industrialist Léon Gaumont. And even though the German pioneers the Skladanowsky brothers (1895) adapted Kodak film to their Bioskop, reducing it from the original 89mm to 55mm, it did not become regular practice. In America, in 1897, a large 63mm format was employed for a single film to record the boxing match between Corbett and Fitzsimmons for the Veriscope Company, with five perforations on each side and a broad rectangular format, similar to future *panoramic* ratios (1:1.75). There were occasional uses of other mega-formats: a British 48mm in Newman's Viventoscope for Blair in 1897, and 60mm by Prestwich in 1898. The same year, the Lumière brothers (with their trusted engineer Carpentier) developed a 73mm film for projection on a very large screen (20m x 16m) which was used during the Paris International Exhibition of 1900. And there was our own Filoteo Alberini, the first creator of an Italian film patent (the Kinetograph, December 21, 1895): from 1897 to the mid-1920s Alberini continued to experiment with 70mm film, using a wide gauge rectangular *panorama* (known as the Panoramico Alberini).

In the following years, further sporadic attempts were made either to increase the definition of the image (the greater the surface, the less enlargement needed to obtain optimal resolution during projection) or to broaden the space for a more spectacular narrative. "I felt that I lacked space for some scenes, that the image, however great it was, was too small for me",[70] wrote Abel Gance, while still at the writing phase of his *Napoleon*. He was indeed prefiguring his need to triple the screen at times, obtaining both hyper-panoramic space and showing different subjects matched in various ways which, using the appropriate colours, at the end became the French flag. André Debrie developed a device for the *triptych* using three cameras and three projectors juxtaposed and synchro-

---

70 In Kevin Brownlow, *Come Gance ha realizzato Napoléon* (original title: *Napoleon: Abel Gance's Classic Film*), Editrice Il Castoro, 2002, p. 137

nised, obtaining a super-screen of unique and exciting vastness (ratio: 1:3.99!!!). Later called Polyvision and then Magirama, this system, which somehow prefigures Cinerama, was used only for this film in 1926 and, though Gance used it for several scenes, he later destroyed them all except for the final one.

The following year, still in France and thanks to the film *Napoleon*,[71] prof. Henri Chrétien formulated a new principle which was to be the basis for a successful progressive development: anamorphosis. Inspired by the studies of Ernst Abbe (1897) he had already designed the Hypergonar, a system of cylindrical lenses that compressed the image laterally. Though this invention was frequently employed even in the USA (as early as 1925 Claude Autant Lara used it experimentally for a short film entitled *Construire un feu*, which passed virtually unnoticed as it was not released until 1929 as a silent film when the sound era was already in full swing), for the moment no one seemed interested in its application in film. It was only in 1953 that Fox began to exploit it under the name of Cinemascope. Indeed, in some ways, it was a veritable Columbus' egg. The basic problem was not "inventing" new formats or systems. Indeed, after sound exploded on the scene, almost all the major companies tried to introduce *large formats*. In 1929, Fox introduced the 70 mm *Grandeur* while Paramount had *Magnafilm* at 56mm. In 1930, Warner produced the 65mm *Vitascope*, there was a 65mm from United Artists and *Realife* from MGM was also 65mm. In 1930, there was even another anamorphic system, the *Fulve Process* by the Englishman George Ford (created together with FW Watson Baker of Watson and Sons). But not only were the times not yet ripe, each cinema would have needed new equipment to screen these new formats just when the great sound revolution had already forced managers to radically refurbish their premises. Therefore, since 35mm versions of the same films were also in distribution, the phenomenon soon faded. Instead, when Fox released *The Robe* in 1953, in a squeezed anamorphic 35mm print, relatively few changes were needed in cinema equipment. In any case, for those who did not want the maximum

71 Vedi Jean-Jacques Meusy, *Un astronomo nel mondo dello Show-Biz, Henri Crétien, padre del Cinemascope*, in "Cinegrafie" 16, Le Mani – Cineteca Bologna, 2003, p. 25

possible results (*Cinemascope* included 4-track magnetic sound) *compatible* copies were made available.

To this day (and in sound systems in particular in recent years), *compatibility* has remained the defining principle in the whole evolution of an industry which had opted, in 1909, for free interchange, if not quite universal standardisation. This observation brings us back to the correct sequence of our story.

From the early 50 feet (approx 17 meters), we moved to 100 feet of celluloid in 1895 *spread* on a glass table larger than 60m x 1m, which was then coated with a layer of emulsion and cut into strips. A continuous system[72] was then introduced which gradually led to the manufacture of increasingly long lengths of film, from 250 feet at the start of the century to 1,000 feet (305 meters) in the early 1900s for positive copies. Even today this measurement identifies the length of the first films, the *one reelers*: at the rate of about 16 feet per second (2 turns of the crank) one reel lasted at most fourteen minutes. The second stage (mentioned in reference to *The Fall of Troy*) led to the *two reelers*, which then became the standard for comic shorts at the beginning of the second decade, to the arrival of the *feature film*, which had no fixed duration and consisted of at least three or four reels. While the *length* of film stock for shooting was, and still is, shorter (even today, with few exceptions, cameras mount 400-foot (120m) magazines[73] with an autonomy of just over 4 minutes, at 24 f/s), already by the 20s Pathé (exceptionally?) had made a continuous *film positif* of 873m (2,865 feet). Both in Europe and in America *film canisters* reached cinemas with prints glued together two by two, making the standard projection reel 600m – at least until the beginning of the 70s

---

72 "These machines have a continuous output, producing about 16 meters of film per hour. In a 24-hour day, 384 m of 55 cm wide film are obtained, which makes 5760 m of film at a width of 3.5 cm. The film is perfectly regular and thickness does not vary even by one hundredth of a millimetre". L. Clément and C. Rivière, *L'industrie du film cinématographique*, p. 6 issue n. 1 of Revue scientifique et technique de l'industrie cinématographique et des industries qui s'y rattachent', Paris, 15 November, 1912: cited in *Les vingt premières années du cinéma français*, PSN-AFRHC1995, p. 66.

73 According to Brian Coe (*The History of the Movie Photography*, Eastview Editions, Westfield 1981, p. 82) the first camera with 400-foot wooden interchangeable external magazine was a Prestwich, which was even fitted with a counter, produced in England as of 1898 (patent dated 18 August, 1898). Coe writes: "The 400-foot magazine soon became established as a standard size".

when this entire length could finally be manufactured both for black & white and colour.

We know that celluloid (i.e.nitrate) is highly flammable and if not properly stored, can spontaneously catch fire even at relatively low temperatures (41°C); it burns intensely and even when immersed in water the combustion continues to produce oxygen, thus feeding itself. Chemically, moreover, celluloid is an unstable material and it begins to deteriorate immediately, albeit very slowly. At first, this compromises the quality of the images but it will ultimately decompose completely. The primary defect was a slight proportional shrinkage (in many cases, as this continues over the years, the material becomes unusable) that forced technicians to design pyramidal teeth for the sprockets that drive the film in the projector. This also explains, as we have already seen, the enormous importance attached to the shape and positioning of the perforations. These *holes* reached their definitive design only in 1924 when the Bell & Howell (BH) system was perfected and adopted for the negative; the rectangular version with rounded corners of the Kodak Standard (KS) was adopted instead for the positive, as it was more resistant to continuous mechanical stress.

Since the number of users continued to grow, the need arose to find a safer, non-flammable support: metal salts were added to the celluloid mixture or immersed in special chemical solutions, but the results were not encouraging. In 1909 an acetate (diacetate) was introduced. Initially, it was more expensive and much less manageable than nitrate, not only regarding shrinkage, but once perfected[74] it was used to manufacture copies for educational purposes in places not equipped to deal with fire (schools, boarding schools, industries, etc.). From the 1920s, it facilitated the development of the so-called reduced formats for amateur or semi-professional use.[75] In 1936, the Belgian company Gevaert introduced

---

74 In France, for a while, it was the only support allowed, though this rule was dropped on the advice of industrialists in the sector, precisely because it was impractical.

75 The main ones: first a 28mm by Pathé (Pathé-KOK) in 1912 and then their 9.5mm in 1922 (Pathé-Baby); followed in 1923 by a 16mm from Kodak; in 1929, back in America thanks to the insight of the Kodel Electric Company in Cincinnati, this 16mm was cut in half to produce 8mm, which was produced, from 1932, by their parent company Kodak. There have been dozens and dozens of "amateur" formats since 1898. But those that really made the history of cinema are the 9.5 mm, 16 mm and 8 mm which at the (*continued overleaf*)

59

stable and safe triacetate for amateur cinema. From 1950 onward, triacetate quickly replaced highly dangerous nitrate all across the globe. However, in certain conditions of temperature and humidity, triacetate also suffers from a destructive phenomenon of chemical decay named the *vinegar syndrome,* in 1993,[76] due to the very strong odour produced during decomposition. Finally, in 1955, the American company Dupont developed polyester (Estar, Cronar, Mylar and other brands); so stable and robust is this material that it literally consumes parts of the projector. Yet, it struggled to impose itself on the market and has only recently been almost universally adopted.

The emulsion, derived from photography (the "opaque and slightly rough" side described by Re), was made of organic gelatin, a suspension of silver salts (bromides, iodides, chlorides – generically, silver halides) that allowed the formation of a latent image that was then developed and fixed. Naturally, it yielded a grey-scale reproduction of a coloured reality based on the negative-positive principle. Like the photography of the time, the emulsion was sensitive to ultraviolet, violet and blue, partially sensitive to yellow and green, but not at all sensitive to red. Optimistically named *orthochromatic* (all paper print material for photography remains orthochromatic and under the classic red light full control can be exercised in the darkroom), it forced directors, costume designers and set designers (when these roles became diversified), to use only tested and controllable colours, or rather, to adopt a range monochromes between black and white in the design and construction of costumes and scenery. This failure to reproduce some colours allowed Méliès, among others, to highlight his ability at sketching: drawing complex forms in pale blue in advance, he would quickly trace them over in black in front of the camera,

behest of Kodak in 1962, became Super 8 (managing to outrun a rival a Japanese consortium linked to Fuji which produced a analogous format of higher handling quality: the single 8). The Pathé-KOK remains invaluable because so many titles that were printed in that short-lived format would otherwise be lost today. But the story of reduced formats is so complex and varied that it is impossible to go into it here.

76 James M. Reilly of the Rochester Institute of Technology coined this term.

thus appearing to be magically and literally a *Dessinateur Express.*[77] As we have already pointed out, it was practically impossible to film using artificial incandescent light since it is essentially based on the red range of the visible spectrum. To prevent "staining" the image with overglow, an "antihalo" layer was soon introduced in a variety of ways, including applying it to the opposite side of the film; it also stopped *curling* which could occur since the emulsion tended to shrink slightly when drying. And even though by 1896 Eastman was already producing two different types of emulsion, one for the negative and the other for the positive, until 1917 there was little diversification between the chemical composition of these two products.

To produce an emulsion that could code all possible colours was becoming indispensable. In 1911, Gaumont planned to develop a new colour system, based on black and white film, that would hopefully be able to reproduce most, if not all, the spectrum. It was thanks to this that Kodak came to produce its *panchromatic* film. After Gaumont's Chronochrome quickly came to an end, panchromatic film struggled to gain popularity being difficult to handle: it was initially rather insensitive and, above all, much more expensive than the regular option. It officially started out with the film *The Headless Horseman*[78] made in the USA in 1922. When Kodak reduced the price of their new negative in 1926 it led to rapid and widespread diffusion. It also allowed for the introduction, upgrading and improvement of incandescent lighting equipment (as an alternative to other sources of lighting). The same year, Kodak also launched an emulsion that made it possible to produce optimal duplicates of original negatives. Until then, to ensure quality copies for the whole market, it was necessary to film the same scene simultaneously with paired cameras, obtaining

---

77 A film deemed lost, n. 37 of the Catalogue, made in summer 1896. Thankfully, we have descriptions from catalogues or contemporary publications of many films that have not been found (unfortunately, more than two thirds).

78 Produced by Sleepy Hollow Corp., directed by Edward D. Venturini, photographed by Ned Van Buren and starring Will Rogers.

two slightly different negatives,[79] one which could be sent out of the country of origin for use abroad.[80] Instead, the duplication of the negative (and soon the positive) allowed, for the multiplication of the *original* with an acceptable loss of quality. In 1928, a panchromatic emulsion sensitive to infrared rays became available which created particular *day-for-night effects,* modifying the true lighting of shots taken during the day. From 1928 onwards, film stock produced in Europe and America gradually became more sensitive and adaptable to lighting and expressive requirements (indeed, Kodak never really enjoyed an absolute monopoly, while remaining dominant on the market, it always encountered strong competitors). In 1931, in Germany, the DIN system was developed to measure the *speed* of the various emulsions available. Over the years these continued to be refined offering greater definition even though sensitivity was constantly being improved.

One last fact, before considering colour: like photography, cinema was born as a negative-positive process, highlighting the possibility of obtaining copies which are the actual products, ephemeral perhaps, but the tangible result of the industrial and economic exploitation of a system. *Reduced* or amateur cinema also originated under the same principle, though in formats that were less successful probably due to the complexity of developing and printing – as we will see later. *Reduced* cinema began to establish itself at the beginning of the 1920s, not only because of improved safety, thanks to the non-flammable base, but also because – alongside Lumière's Autochrome, the first reliable natural colour system, between 1914 and 1916 – Kodak began to research a reversible black and white. In other words, a system that made the negative directly positive, thus obtaining a single original that the non-professional could handle (processing it and of course assembling it) after the appropriate laboratory operations had been carried out. Both Pathé and Kodak (the previous year the former had

79 Certain restorations today are problematic: comparing surviving copies it is often impossible to attempt a reconstruction given the different angles of certain frames. For the record, *double* cameras, in the sense that a single crank operated two independent but coupled mechanisms, were used over a period of time, allowing for continuous and almost identical filming.

80 Méliès was a precursor also in this. In November 1902, he opened the American branch of his Star Films for which he prepared original negatives.

already released reduced 9.5mm films, the latter started with 16mm) entered the market in 1923 with similar systems, giving birth to a "do it yourself" cinema. The training ground where amateurs began to experiment was *reversible* film stock, both in America and Europe, including the first colour systems based on chemical reactions.

The Camera

With a metal heart of the highest mechanical craftsmanship, encased in a precious wooden body, preferably mahogany, it is almost pointless to reiterate that from the outset – the very first Lumière Cinematograph – the cine camera has always been a device imbued with charm, elegance and functionality. It would be neither simple nor useful to attempt to map or chronicle the dozens of cameras that came on the market in Europe and America during the early years of cinema. We know they were based on a variety of intermittent drive systems, such as the *claw*, the *eccentric cam* and, even *the Maltese cross* (introduced by the German Oskar Meßter in 1896). Initially, it was capable of exposing the maximum available length of film (50 feet), which was driven thanks to "do it yourself" perforations. Since the *claw* was destined to be the winning mechanism, to understand how filming systems were refined, we will start from the Cinematograph. The crank that drove the film yielded eight frames at every rotation. The cameraman had to turn the crank two times per second – one hundred and twenty per minute – thus capturing 16 frames per second, the basic number necessary to record "life as it is". The only problem was to maintain a steady speed: tradition has it that this was done mentally following the rhythm of a song.[81] Of course it soon became apparent (it was enough to watch an Edison film on a projector rather than through the Kinetoscope) that increasing the speed while shooting and then projecting at normal speed slowed down the action, while filming slower instead produced an amusing acceleration: thus two of the first and simplest *tricks*, or *special effects* as we call them today, were discovered almost

---

81 Years ago a search was initiated to identify the favourite tune used in each country: the outcome is unknown.

immediately. In the Cinematograph the crank was at the back of the machine, instead, in all subsequent models it was found more advantageous to set it on the right side, leaving the other hand free, to manage the mounting head, for example. The crank operated the *claw* which dragged the frame downwards and set it in position as it went up to hook the next frame. A rotating shutter, synchronised with the claw, allowed the film to be exposed when it was immobile and blocked the light while a new frame scrolled into position. The surface of the shutter (two superimposable metal blades) could be modified, increasing or decreasing the amount of incoming light, regardless of the diaphragm selected on the lens. Initially, this operation needed to be done before every shot, but later, towards the end of the first decade, it became possible to intervene while the camera was running. The adjustable shutter is still a key element in the most advanced cameras: it compensates for deformed lighting in an imperceptible manner (when panning or tracking from an interior to an exterior or vice versa, or moving from one ambiance to another); or makes the best use of the lens' depth of field which varies depending on diaphragm aperture (plus the focus in the space framed and vice versa).[82] At the time, however, external manipulation of the adjustable shutter simplified what had only been previously possible by adjusting the lens diaphragm, in other words progressively increasing or reducing incoming light, a fundamental procedure for *special effects*. For example, gradually closing the diaphragm, then rewinding to a precise point on the film and filming again with a similar gradual opening produced a *cross-fade*: a soft and nuanced transition from one image to another. Up until the mid-twenties, this effect, but also the more complex matte and counter matte effects that assembled series of different shots into

---

82 This is a fundamental rule in photography. However, while in photography shutter speed is variable, in cinema it must remain constant. Within certain limits, the adjustable shutter manages to make up for this necessity, also and above all because, while photography is based for the most part on natural light, cinema can always reinforce lighting artificially. Thanks to the application of this rule, and the shrewd management of lenses with different focal lengths, *deep focus* effects can be obtained (sharply focused images from the foreground through to the background) as in the celebrated film *Citizen Kane* by Orson Welles (1941). Contrary to some accounts, it was not filmed using special lenses (which never existed ...), but only by genially *compensating* focal length, variable shutter and diaphragm in accordance with artificial light.

a single frame, were achieved exclusively on the original negative that was exposed, rewound and re-exposed as many times as necessary. The end result could only be seen after development and if there were issues or obvious failures, the entire procedure had to be repeated. It was sufficient to turn the crank in the opposite direction (*rewind*), ensuring the flow of light was shut off. A similar procedure was used to film reverse action (the swimmer coming out of the water and up to the diving board, a classic!),[83] going backwards some misframing was inevitable as the *claw's* altered alignment with the perforations would shift the position of the interline. To identify the starting point for each effect – which, necessarily, had to be done in the dark – a small thread was tied to the perforation so that it could be located again by touch[84] (alternatively, and more simply, many cameras could punch small holes in the film from the outside). Initially, duration was gauged by counting the number of crank rotations. But in the early years of the 20th century, equipment with inbuilt counters came on the market, thus, as well as the speed and a rough count of film length, it also became possible to count single frames.

And while all of this started, more or less, at the outset of the first decade of the 20th century, the optical printer become available only much later[85] – in America with Linwood Dunn in 1928 and in Europe with André Debrie in 1929 (real marketing began several years later, in Europe as late as 1936). Thanks to Debrie it took on a name in many languages that now completely identifies it: *truka* (translator's note: though called optical printer in English, in Italian it is generally referred to as *truca*). This device, which combines a projector with a camera, allowed for the composition

---

83 In his film *The Cameraman* (1928), Buster Keaton plays on these procedures to convey the clumsiness of an apprentice cameraman. In the same period however (see Dziga Vertov's *The Man with the Movie Camera*, 1929), they were fundamental to the wilful technical and linguistic transgressions of the avant-garde.

84 It is a system still in use for printing extracts, the *threads* help to locate a precise point in complete darkness.

85 According to Barry Salt (*Film Style and Technology, History and Analysis*, Starword, London, 1983–1992), in England, at the beginning of the 20th century, Cecil Hepworth had already developed and used a rudimentary prototype of the *optical printer* called the *projection printer*. Indeed, a title printer was used over the following years for titles and captions, it was composed of a magic lantern that projected the text from a photographic plate directly on the negative (Colin Bennett, *The Handbook of Kinematography*, London 1913, p. 84).

and control of scenes derived from multiple sources, when filming had already been completed – thus expanding the range of invention infinitely. Nevertheless, as an alternative to the adjustable shutter, accessories mounted in front of the lens for other simple *live* effects soon became available.

Continuing with our description of the Cinematograph, we now need to introduce the lenses which were set in front of the shutter in line with the film gate: the opening onto the vertical corridor through which the film is channelled, two springs control pressure plates on the sides where the perforations are, so as to maintain the most stable alignment possible as the film moves. The first lenses used by the Lumière brothers did not carry any specifications. The standard lens marketed shortly afterwards, in 1897, was a 54mm Zeiss with an aperture of 6.5 (was this design already a *planar*[86]?), a lens that was defined as *normal*[87] as it rendered an image very close to the vision of the human eye. And even if various manufacturers were soon able to design brighter lenses (the Zeiss *Tessar*, f:3.5, was available as of 1903), for that time precise focus on every plane remained fundamental and a medium aperture could only help in obtaining nicely defined images. It is no coincidence that, among the characteristics of a camera described in a Pathé catalogue dated 1903, we read: "The lens [another Zeiss, *ed*] always remains in focus from 5 meters to infinity, thus the cameraman does not have to regulate focus, undeniably a very delicate operation".[88]

This was probably not so much because the lenses were actually set on a *fixed focus* but because the relative brightness guaranteed stability of definition beyond a certain technically defined *hyperfocal* distance (i.e. the minimum focal distance from which the depth of field extends to infinity). This rapid progress in the development of lenses for cine cameras was more an issue of compensating for

86 "A lens designed by P. Rudolph of Zeiss in 1896, based on the Gauss scheme. It was characterised by a large opening, a good field plane and an excellent spherical aberration correction". Calvenzi – Celentano – Lazzarin, *Il dizionario della fotografia*, Cesco Capanna Editore, Rome 1985 p. 184.

87 In actual fact, compared to the diagonal (24 x 18mm) *normal* 35mm film is closer to 30mm than to 50mm; but in practice it has always been used and the 50mm is still used.

88 Anciens Établissements Pathé Frères, *Cinématographe Pathé, Appareil à prise de vue*, 1903, p. 54.

aberrations (a specialist subject that is difficult to synthesise here) rather than that of brightness which, as we have said, would have further complicated the activity of the cameraman who was primarily interested in obtaining perfectly *focused* images. Especially since the manuals of the time, at the start of the second decade, rightly defined the lenses on the market (in addition to Zeiss, Voitgländer, Steinheil and Duplonich) as *very fast*, since they already offered apertures close to 3.5[89] and focal lengths that already widened the field without deforming it (the 35mm, wide angle), or narrowed it (by today's standard) with an average telephoto lens (the 75mm) which gradually became the main lens for *close-ups*.

To control the frame, the Cinematograph was soon equipped with a "telescopic optical system (with a diverging and a converging lens) [...] affected by some parallax error"[90] also known as a *Galilean viewfinder* – again clearly borrowed from photography again. Parallax is the

> difference between the actual scene filmed and what appears framed. It occurs in cameras [...] where the optical axis of the sighting system does not coincide with that of the shooting lens, for example in the Galilean viewfinder or a twin-lens reflex. The shorter the shooting distance the greater the error.[91]

Transforming photographic terminology somewhat, the *twin-lens reflex* system was described in the 1903 Pathé manual[92] as a "viewfinder placed at the front of the device, next to the lens, which allows the cameraman to view what is happening within the frame of action". It is important to consider this description, because the subsequent model in 1905 replaced the small prism in the viewfinder with a more precise system where a second lens was inserted into the camera body above the shooting lens which, thanks again to a prism, ensured a less complex and continuous control of shooting in a viewfinder set on the side, above the

89 In Colin N. Bennett's *The Handbook of Kinematography*, published in London in 1913, a 3-inch Dallmeyer is mentioned that had an aperture of f: 1.9 which was amazing for the time.

90 Calvenzi – Celentano – Lazzarin, *Il dizionario della fotografia,* cit. p. 162.

91 Ibidem p. 178.

92 Anciens Établissements Pathé Frères, *Cinématographe Pathé,* cit. p. 52.

crank. However, even in this case, it was still approximate. Therefore, to be sure of the framing, the shot needed to be composed
before loading the film, inserting a small piece of "frosted celluloid
or tracing paper",[93] or later a small frosted glass, into the pressure
plate of the film gate which could capture the frame as it was in
the lens, obviously upside down. Or, later, making appropriate
modifications to the camera body so as to attach a viewfinder
with an optical crystal that read the virtual image reproduced by
the lens, though always before inserting the negative. The usual
practice was the Galilean viewfinder coupled with experience to
compensate for data that could not be gauged objectively. Only
much later, from the 1930s, was a solution found that allowed
the cameraman to control every moment of every shot with absolute
precision, especially when different focal lenses were adopted with
expressive qualities that could still be simulated in the Galilean
viewfinder. With the evolution of shooting technology, different
focal lenses began to be set in rotating turrets that allowed them
to be changed quickly and precisely.

This accessory was probably invented in America but it was soon
adopted by other manufacturers (especially by Debrie in France,
towards the end of the 1910s). The camera that was considered
the most reliable for years, at least in America, was developed
from an important patent. Around 1912, Bell and Howell came
up with an intermittent mechanism that integrated the action of
the *claw* with *register pins* that held the film in a precise position
during exposure, resulting in perfectly steady images. The Bell &
Howell 2709 was born, the body was no longer made of wood
but of cast aluminium, and it prefigured later equipment even in
the management of accessories, materials and its appearance. Even
the twin compartment magazines, also made of metal, and their
total capacity of 1000 feet (305 meters): two round containers
compacted into a single body, with the film stock running from
one side to the other as it was exposed. The system was gradually
adopted universally as it allowed for efficient and rapid loading.
Returning for the last time to the Lumière brothers' Cinematograph, we again find a true insight. Indeed, from the very

93 FP Liesegang, *Il cinematografo*, cit. p. 343 s.

beginning those 50 feet of film were housed in a small wooden box that was easily replaceable, and, once exposed, rolled into a metal container inside the camera. With the availability of greater lengths of film, cameras were equipped with two wooden cartridges: one full and one, obviously, empty. The capacity was initially 60 meters, but this was soon increased to the standard 120 meters still in use today. The positioning of these magazines varied according to the type of camera: the simplest had them inside, the camera body remained unchanged – a regular parallelepiped; the more complex ones had them attached outside, prefiguring the form and function of the B&H 2709. Of course, for some time various sprockets had already been installed before and after the intermittent motion to guide the film gently and safely inside the camera, avoiding tearing or jamming (called *salad*, in Italian jargon).

In 1916, writing about effects obtained using *double or multiple combination shots and mattes*, Vittorio Mariani commented:

> These effects are achieved by blinding out a section of the film gate so that only part of the frame is exposed. The film is then rewound, and the other part of the film gate is blinded and a second shot is filmed. In this way, two, three or more scenes can be filmed on the same frames. There are also special mattes, which, when placed before the aperture, make the scene appear as if through a keyhole or binoculars, etc.[94]

As we have already said, by 1916 a widely used feature, which had started in America,[95] had become pinpointing a subject by outlining it with round, vertical or even completely irregular matte, either fixed or mobile, especially closing in on or opening out from a given position, foreshadowing an effect similar to that achieved nowadays by the zoom. For *double and multiple combinations shots*, the preferred place to position these differently shaped *mattes* (and corresponding counter-mattes, obviously) was on the film gate, inside the camera therefore, on the film path where the light filters through the lens. Before the advent of the optical

94 V. Mariani, *Guida pratica della cinematografia*, Ulrico Hoepli 1916, p. 121.

95 "A few years ago, and it is a fashion that has come from America, it has become a habit to start scenes, with a black screen, on which the image appears as if from a point that opens gradually". Leopold Lobel, *La technique cinématographique,* Dunod Editeur, Paris 1922, p. 162.

printer, the ease with which such operations could be carried out was a particularly sought-after feature in certain cameras. For such functions, especially for the above-mentioned mattes, a systems of slots was created in front of the lens hood (which acted as a shield from incidental light) that could hold steady items such as an iris controlled from the outside for openings and closures, or a variety of cardboard or foil masks (including binoculars, keyhole holes, etc.) that were superimposed on the image. Let us recall a few images, such as the smooth cornered rectangle that outlines the charging Ku Klux Klan in *Birth of a Nation* (which seems to prefigure the spectacular spaces similar to CinemaScope), or the often coherently jagged mattes used in Robert Wiene's impressionistic *The Cabinet of Dr. Caligari* (1919–1920), or the *split screen*, showing contemporaneous or multiple actions taking place in different places, such as Williamson's *Are You There?* (1901), showing two characters in a phone conversation.

Today these slots are used for filters that colour or attenuate the diffusion of light (a blinding sky for example) but only in specific areas of the image, or else lenses that magnifying parts of the image so that elements in the foreground can coexist in a frame where the focus is on a very distant background.

Special high-speed cameras began to be marketed in the 1920s, particularly in the field of scientific research where cinema was starting to be regarded as an objective instrument for gathering data. The first mechanisms with a Maltese cross in an oil capsule could not exceed 120 f/s. To achieve greater speed, intermittent movement had to be eliminated, the film proceeded in continuous motion and the frames were exposed by synchronising the negative with a rotating mirror drum, which, on principle (*optical compensation*), recalled Reynaud's Praxinoscope. By the mid twenties, Lucien Bull's *caméra à grande vitesse* could film at 25,000 f/s illuminating the subject with the aid of continuous electric sparks.[96]

---

96 Obtained by using a Ruhmkorff coil which functioning like a shutter thanks to the high frequency of alternating light and dark.

Colour

Colour was practically imposed on cinema, yet again, by analogy with photography. From the outset, colour had been part of Magic Lantern shows. Then, as photography grew in popularity, it became possible to give added value to glass positives by colouring them, depending on the subject, with transparent paints such as lacquers, watercolours and organic varnishes, improperly referred to as anilines (however, for convenience we will continue to use this name). Indeed, this had already been done with the metal supports of daguerreotypes and on printed paper. Moreover, images celebrating events and anniversaries, whether artistic or not, had almost always been coloured, and even monochromes were cast in colour. The era of black and white began with the spread of photography and its reproduction in the periodical press which, as soon as it could (and long before photography *tout court*), began to recreate colour through the use of several *shots* in black and white codified through filters corresponding to the three print colours (cyan, magenta and yellow). This tricolour process[97] had already been used in lantern shows: simultaneous and superimposed projections of three negative transparencies from three sources in the dominant colours (blue, red, green).[98] We shall see how the first attempts at colour in cinema were based on these two principles. But let us not get ahead of ourselves. The first advertisement for a coloured film appeared in "The Era" on April 8, 1896, the film was *Eastern Dance* by the Englishman R. W. Paul and was shown at the Alhambra in London. However, given the nature of commercial relationships at that time, this may have been a screening of Edison's famous *Serpentine Dance*, as described in the "New York Herald" on May 3, 1896 (it was the first screening that employed a Vitascope projector). That was, moreover, a "recycled" film shot between 1894 and 1895 with the dancer Annabelle Whitford Moore,[99] who had made at least three similarly titled films in

---

97 In 1855, Scottish physicist James Clerk Maxwell postulated that three colours were enough to reconstruct the entire spectrum using an additive system based on the primary colours. He proved this six years later.

98 It might seem like a contradiction to speak of red when dealing with orthochromatic emulsions. It was later understood that sensitivity to ultraviolet rays, however, allowed for a certain approximation to red in the first colour procedures.

99 See C. Musser, *Edison Motion Pictures...*, cit., pp. 111, 173 and 188.

Edison's Black Maria over the same period. The novelty was the addition of colour to the positive, though coloured films for the Kinetoscope had been made even earlier.[100] It seems that the idea of adding colour came from the fact that this *serpentine dance* (originally created by dancer Loïe Fuller[101] and copied by Annabelle) was performed in a vaporous white dress that flowed evocatively and harmoniously, rising and falling in the air, while illuminated by beams of coloured light. The wife of one Edmund Kuhn, a photographer at the Edison laboratories, applied the various "aniline" colours to the gelatine with cotton swabs and brushes. Lacquers could not be used as celluloid was flexible.

In what seems to have been the first hand-coloured film, all the same reference elements of this newly-born medium continue to combine: theatre, photography and cinema. For the record, coloured *serpentine dances* multiplied in those early years as different versions of the subject were shot by all the film producers since it continued to guarantee success. It might even be considered a forerunner of the Futurists' *chromatic dynamism*. One of the last and most extraordinary examples of bright, spectacular film colourings is the finale of *Le Farfalle*, a 192m film produced by the Roman company Cines in February 1908, based on a live show and distributed with its own musical commentary. Was the *Manifesto of Futurism* published in France a year later just a coincidence? Or had cinema influenced the collective imagination, like a steady drop of water wearing down a marble slab, gradually leading to new hypotheses and certainties in parallel creative fields? We will never know, but it seems more than legitimate to ask.

Again, Mariani explains:

> *Colouring by brush* – This method was used by some and was the first adopted in cinematography. It was not difficult. Within a month, girls could learn how to do it correctly. [...] The colours used were light yellow,

100 The first available coloured copy was probably on April 14, 1894 at the Holland Brothers Kinetoscope Parlor, 1155 Broadway, New York (Fred E. Basten *Glorious Technicolor*, AS Barnes and Co. Inc. Cranbury, NJ / Thomas Yoseloff Ltd, London, 1980, p. 13). As was the practice at the time, a positive a paper print was filed at the Library of Congress for Copyright (which version?), but only in 1897.

101 Loie Fuller (1862–1928) worked in revues and variety in America and Europe, and did not disdain appearing in the circus. She introduced very interesting innovations in lighting and stage effects.

orange and blue, then green, red and purple, but always in pale shades. It was done by placing the film on a background light which revealed the outline of the image. Output ranged from 4 to 5 meters per day and cost, according to average pay in Italy, 0.30 lire per meter. Nonetheless, as it was expensive and slow, the process was dropped.[102]

Harold Brown confirms:

> Illuminated from below, the film was moved forward, frame by frame, using a pedal. The colourist observed each frame through a magnifying glass and proceeded as follows: dipping a brush in the required colour, they would paint a section on the first frame, then press the pedal and paint the corresponding section of the next frame and so on until the scene was completed.[103]

These coloured films were like a multiplication of small miniatures therefore, and, given the short average length, they could be sold at a higher price as they were more impressive than their black and white counterparts. The use of a single coloured element to enhance aesthetics and function was sometimes brilliant, explosions for example (as cinema was silent, so to convey that a gun had not misfired, a little cloud was added and it was even better coloured ...), or the red hooded dress worn by a railway worker's daughter in Porter's *The Great Train Robbery*. Or in Méliès' *Le raid Paris-Monte-Carlo en deux heures* (1905) where only the automobile which undertakes this extraordinary enterprise (whether a cutout or a miniature) is coloured red. Though, we could quite likely[104] come across another copy of the same film with more colours, and even – just a hypothesis – with the car in a different colour. The final product was often uneven, random and sloppy, probably also due to the above-mentioned expense. The aniline colours often spread outside the intended contours of persons, clothing or objects, creating a disturbing flicker. The general quality of care taken could not be compared the work at Mme Thuiller's legendary Parisian workshop, active up until the 1920s, to which Méliès constantly entrusted the superb colouring

102 V. Mariani, *Guida pratica ...*, cit., P. 194.

103 H. Brown *Tecniche di colorazione a mano e a pochoir*, "Griffithiana", 29–30 September 1987, p. 72.

104 *Essai de reconstitution du chambre français de la Star-film*, Center National de la Cinématographie, Paris 1981, p. 229.

of his films. Thus, around 1906, on the heels of popular prints, postcards and fabrics, Pathé adopted the *stencil* system[105] at their Vincennes facilities. Yet again, Vittorio Mariani explains:

> *Matrix colouring* – Imagine that we wanted to colour the film using three colours: A, B and C. To apply them, three positives are printed and matrices cut out corresponding to the respective portions to be coloured. The matrix for A is then placed on the positive film, and, frame by frame, the portions left uncovered by the matrix are coloured. The matrix is then removed and the process repeated for the other colours.[106]

Of course, it was a very complex and delicate operation as it was initially done by hand, not only the cutting, frame by frame, but also in the application of dyes with a brush, sponge or pad. Therefore, the procedure (advertised as Pathécolor) was soon mechanised. The matrices were cut using a pantograph: frame by frame, the areas to be cut were identified on an enlarged image on frosted glass and cut with a knife on a second copy of the film perfectly synchronised with the first projection (thanks to the pantograph, movement at least four times finer could be attained). The process was repeated for each colour, reaching up to an exceptional maximum of seven colours. Then, using one matrix at a time, placed exactly on top of the black and white positive, brushes, rollers or other increasingly automated systems (there were various patents) applied the specific colour on the uncovered portion of gelatin. Sometimes, final touches were applied by hand on each copy. From Pathé, the *stencil* system spread, using similar methods, especially through France and Italy. It could be found in fantasy films but also, and above all, in Pathé's immense repertoire of real life documents – in a style we might define as hyper-realistic – recording lifestyles, habits and customs from every part of the world, focusing particularly on exotic and distant countries. As film length extended, the *stencil* technique was also used in feature films up until the beginning of the 30s.[107] Like other colour

---

105 This was a singular spin-off from the 19th century textile industry. In addition to colour printing procedures, this sector is responsible for the introduction of punch cards, conceptually the precursors of mechanical calculators, and, laterally, the development of the first computers.

106 V. Mariani, *Guida pratica ...*, cit., p. 194.

107 For example, in the film *Les Gaietés de l'escadron* by Maurice Tourner, produced by Pathé-Natan in 1932.

systems though, sometimes only a few shots or sequences were coloured – scenes that required spectacular effect. Not very many period copies of feature films coloured with the *stencil* technique have survived, but it is worth recalling at least Alfred Machin's *Maudite soit la guerre* produced in France in 1913 and Augusto Genina's *Cirano di Bergerac* made in Italy in 1922.[108]

It is also worth mentioning an anomalous, handcrafted method developed by Max Handschiegl and used exclusively (though an alternative) by Cecil B. DeMille between 1916 and 1927 (it is also known as the Wyckoff-DeMille process, after DeMille's trusted cameraman). This method produced printing matrices using *internegatives* obtained through complex chemical procedures. It was a process analogous to lithography and transferred colours that were similar to manual or *stencil* colours onto the black and white positive:

> While Handschiegl's images still resembled those of early cinema, their pastel colours had a much higher transparency and luminosity that lent an atmospheric quality to objects and spaces while leaving volumes intact.[109]

As it was a particularly delicate operation; the inventor's death ended any further use of this process.

However, though in 1909 "it was very convenient to colour films using a rotating disc with a variety of coloured glasses set in the projector behind the film gate"[110] – an operation carried out *directly* in the projection booth – the actual colours that accompanied the entire silent era were based on dominant colours (like light filtered through coloured glass), and were quite a different matter.

According to Re:

> There are three species of film: Natural or black, toned, and coloured. The natural or black are like photographs – the toned ones are printed on films of various colours – and the coloured ones, instead, are painted by hand

108 Both have undergone careful and interesting restorations.

109 Paolo Cherchi Usai, "Le nitrate Mécanique", in *La couleur en Cinéma*, Mazzotta/Cinémathèque Française, 1995, p. 102.

110 FP Liesegang, *Il cinematografo...*, cit., p. 271. In the 1920s, this very simple device was to become an accessory in amateur projectors marketed by Pathé. Pathé, however, also adapted the *stencil* procedure for copies in 9.5 mm format sold or rented for home screening.

[...]. Natural films are unanimously considered the best because they are more artistic and reproduce the most minute details. Those that have been toned are the nicest, and the most impressive for images such as fires, the effects of the sea, nighttime or twilight, etc. but they tend to be dark [...].[111]

In recent years, the most problematic aspect in the rediscovery of the cinema of this period is this use of colour in commercial cinema, which was an ever more frequent and therefore less expensive phenomenon. Thanks to a growing interest (aided by the indispensable complicity of television and greatly enhanced by video recording) many archives have returned to the original colour copies in storage, which had been reprinted earlier exclusively in *black and white*, thus something more important than mere "charm" has been discovered in the systematic use of coloured monochrome in the silent era. Monochrome was initially used because it was less expensive than manual or *stencil* colouring, and it was often used as a complement to the "natural or black" scenes described by Re, since varying the colour in individual scenes enhanced the content. It started, of course, by seeking effects (red for fires, light blue for the sea, dark blue for night, pink or purple for twilight), but then it went on systematically to amber for interiors, exteriors were sometimes yellow and sometimes orange (for the sun), green for vegetation, and when the drama was high, the most "natural" black and white. They played with warm-cold tones to contrast internal-external passages and vice versa and also with the sudden switching on or off of light sources.

It was akin to what was possible in photography at that time (this parallel is constant) but without the excess aestheticism or technological and formal refinement linked to painting.[112] Three techniques were adopted for colour in cinema: *imbibition* (or tinting), *toning* and *mordant toning*.

111 G. Re, *Il cinematografo ...*, cit. p. 57.

112 "it should be noted that *Pictorialism* stemmed from research into the artistry of photography, and was promoted due to a negative attitude towards the massification of photography. Every effort was made to make photography more complex and personal, also through the application of new printing procedures. It had the prerogative, or the ambition at least, of rendering the photograph more like a drawing or engraving [...] new printing techniques [...] allowed for velvety images, with the appearance of charcoal or sanguine, the pigments that could be mixed with the photosensitive emulsion were available in a great variety of colours". Italo Zannier *Storia e tecnica della fotografia*, Editori Laterza, Rome-Bari 1984, p. 136 s.

Imbibition was initially carried out by brushing entire sections of positive film. Later, to obtain greater uniformity and faster processing, the whole film was immersed in coloured solutions, lending a homogeneous dominance of the chosen colour to the entire surface, including the perforations. Black portions of the image remained unaltered, while the various greys yielded intermediate shades. In 1912, Gevaert in Belgium began to produce pre-coloured films, while Kodak only began to market them in 1921 offering nine colours: orange, amber, light amber, yellow, pink, red, green, blue and light blue. At the end of the 20s, they expanded their range with another eight colours, many with evocative names.

Toning, however, was a more complex operation that involved a chemical transformation of the silver into a derivative salt and then into a toned positive. All blacks and greys ranged from varying shades of the chosen colour to transparent where the emulsion has been completely dissolved during development (becoming white on the screen). Since the procedures were complex and dangerous because of the reactants employed, few "colours" were possible: sepia, blue, green, red and orange. *Mordant toning* was even more complex and yielded similar results but allowed for a wider range of colours.

> Very attractive effects were obtained by carrying out imbibition after toning. Some of the most popular toned colourings were: Blue toning and pink imbibition which was excellent for marine effects turning blue to purple. Blue toning and yellow imbibition was good for green landscapes, whites became yellow. Blue toning and orange imbibition gave the same results as the previous one above.[113]

Naturally, over time, *imbibition* was also replaced by *pre-coloured positives*, and certain atmospheres were obtained by further enriching imbibition and/or toning and *retouching* them with *stencils*. Among the works that have come down to us, different colourings can found for the same film, this may have depended (but not necessarily) on perceived variations in the culture, tastes and technological practices in different markets. The circulation of films without added colour, instead, can be linked to an objective lack of resources, or even actual economic hardship, rather than to

113 V. Mariani, *Guida Pratica...*, cit., p. 161.

artistic choices. We could say that copies of the same film, rather than the film in itself, tell their own personal and private stories (provided you have the documents).

Since each scene required different colours, the organisation of work in development and printing reflected the needs of colouring.

For years many researchers had been engaged, more or less successfully, in the quest for *natural* photographic colours, attempts had also been made to transfer these discoveries and principles to the developing film industry: below we will only deal with the fundamental stages of this continuous experimentation. We have already mentioned the additive tricolour system used in the Magic Lantern shows: three monochromes projected simultaneously. The German H. Isensee was the first to follow this path (his patent is dated December 17, 1897).[114] His idea was to obtain "a rapid sequence of red, green and blue images on the screen, corresponding to negatives taken using rays of these colours". Straddled between photography and cinema (movement, though not explicitly mentioned, was implicit in the need for temporal succession), the invention had an eccentrically positioned rotating disk with the three colours (red, green, blue) in front of the lens of a "*standard camera*" allowing both the filming and projection of three black and white "photographic shots" codified to the relative colours. While in principle the intuition was correct, its technical solution was highly problematic. The Englishman William Friese-Greene attempted a similar approach with equal difficulty and lack of success. From 1898, Friese-Greene, like many other inventors, tried to overcome issues with brightness, perception (*pulsing* on the screen), speed in filming and projection – and consequent optical and mechanical issues – trying the most diverse methods (prisms, direct colours on the film, filming and screening with several cameras/projectors, etc.). The same journey was undertaken, and only partly concluded, in an English patent filed by F. Marshall Lee and Edward R. Turner, dated March 22, 1899. With a shutter that had three coloured filters three similar black and white images

114 Many thanks to Martin Koerber from the Berlin Film Museum who discovered the original document at the Patent Office: n. 98799, Klasse 57: Photographie, Vorrichtung zur Darstellung farbiger lebender Photographieen.

were filmed in sequence, each one therefore with the relative chromatic filtering. A projector equipped with three lenses and a triple gate was then used, its axis set so that the three frames were simultaneously superimposed on the screen. A rotating shutter allowed each coloured monochrome to be projected separately on the screen so that the rapid overlap of the three images meant that natural colour would be perceived. The prototype was actually built and test films on 38mm film were shot between 1901 and 1902, but this understandably difficult experimentation failed to go much further, also due to Turner's demise. The patent was then taken over by Charles Urban, who had arrived in Britain as an Edison representative and soon became one of the most dynamic and enterprising industrialists in the field. Urban brought in the "pioneer" George Albert Smith who came up with a solution in 1906. Smith simplified the system by adopting only two colours (red and green, or rather, red-orange and blue-green), yielding a sufficiently acceptable reproduction of reality for the time.[115] Camera and projector (both with two coloured rotary filters attached to the shutter) ran at 32f/s, allowing for two similar but alternating images every sixteenth of a second, which was rapid enough to be amalgamated in the viewer's perception. Patented in November 1906, Kinemacolor was presented to the Royal Society of Arts on December 9, 1908 and was commercially released the following February. It yielded positive results for years around the world especially in documenting current events (such as *The Durbar at Delhi* in 1911, the coronation of George VI as Emperor of India). However, for satisfactory screenings specific equipment was necessary since the system was incompatible with the projectors in common use.

This duotone system, reworked in all its possible and imaginable forms up until the 50s, was to be one of the most persistent avenues of research taken in the attempt to provide *natural* colours in cinema. But we will return to that later, in the meantime, in 1911, Gaumont solved the three colour additive problem and patented the first effective, though complex, system. Let us

---

115 A fundamental principle of progress: until a system is perfected, the best thing available is what one has. Otherwise, it would be difficult to understand our great-grandparents' and grandparents' often enthusiastic acceptance of obviously rudimentary early discoveries.

remember that it was precisely for the Gaumont Chronochrome that Eastman researched and manufactured the first panchromatic emulsion and, what is more, on a non-flammable support. Chrono-chrome came in an unusual format, reduced one quarter lower than the standard 4/3, foreshadowing what would be called *wide-screen* in the 50s (though this new ratio was actually 1:1.71). In shooting and in projection, it managed three frames at a time, each one 14mm instead of 18 (consequently, it engaged three perforations per frame instead of four). This decision to shorten the segment of film was dictated by mechanics and stability, but more importantly it reduced the surface of the three images that needed to be superimposed in projection so as to reconstruct the colour – an attempt to minimise the parallax effect caused by very slight differences in angle while filming. Both camera and projector had triple lenses each one equipped with a coloured filter (red, green and blue). The central lens of the projector was fixed, while the other two, above and below, could be micrometrically adjusted to keep the three frames in register, even during screening. Despite some persistent flaws, *Chronochrome* was presented in 1912 and met with remarkable public success. Complex equipment was needed and only certain venues (in Paris, London and New York) were equipped to screen these films (often conceived to take advantage of the extraordinary quality of this colour reproduction – documentaries in particular, from real life events). It soon became known as *Gaumont-Color*. Following a break (the First World War), it was taken up again in 1919, but was finally abandoned a few years later.

The recent discovery of many original negatives at George Eastman House, has allowed all three monochromes to be reassembled into single negatives for contemporary use with very charming results. In essence, *Gaumont-Color* anticipated what was to be the best colour system developed for the cinema in the 30s: *Technicolor tripack*. The concept behind *Technicolor* took form in those years, employing the dichromatic system which, as we have already said, was constantly being reinvented in the most diverse variants. For example, colouring the positive frames alternately, thus eliminating coloured filters in projection (*Biocolour*, 1911); compressing the two images into the space of a single frame and then using a prism to superimpose and colour them in projection (*Colcin* film, 1913); using a prism to simultaneously deflect light from a single lens and expose two negatives side by side on a double-width film with three rows of perforations, one central of course (the first phase of *Cinechrome*, dating back to 1914).

It was precisely on this last idea (*beam-splitter – ray division*) that, Herbert Kalmus, Daniel Frost Comstock and W Burton Wescott founded the Technicolor Motion Picture Corporation in a railway wagon in Boston, in 1915. They built a camera that could film two identical but offset frames through a single lens, thanks to a prism, coded according to the two dominant colours. Unlike other systems described above, the two images were identical since they were obtained from a single source. The lens and mechanics were similar in the projector. However, having made a pilot film in 1917 (*The Gulf Between*) and having taken it on the road as a demonstration (the train-laboratory ...), Kalmus came to realise that the corrections necessary during screenings called for a pro-jectionist who was a cross between a scientist and an acrobat. This was the moment when the additive colour process was abandoned in favour of the subtractive process.

To be clear, the process had to be able to transfer the colour image directly on the film by automating, we might say, what was already being done through manual and *stencil colouring*. Thanks to Arturo Hernandez-Mejia we have the *Colorgraph* (de-veloped between 1911 and 1912 and patented in 1916), the first known subtractive system which was still based on exposing the usual two negatives coded red and green. They had to be mirror images as they were printed on a *duplitised* positive film (with emulsion on both sides). Once processed, the images were colour toned in their complementary colour, so that when the light finally passing through it *subtracted* from the sum of the two shades reproducing the result on the screen. This *duplitised* and coloured positive film was to be the basic principle on which many other researchers exercised their ingenuity, focusing particularly on per-fecting yield and definition during filming.

We do not have sufficient space here to investigate other inventions developed over time, some even managed to reach the production stage. We should mention the *lenticular*[116] additive system that needed a support covered in cylindrical protuberances which, thanks to refraction, proportionally coded the emulsion according to the amount of coloured light entering through a striped green, red and blue filter placed in front of the lens. Obviously, the filter had also to be used when projecting the positive. Conceived by Berthon in 1909, it underwent further improvements, and in the late 1920s it became Kodak's first colour system on the amateur market. And we should also mention the *mosaic process*[117] which had a regular pattern composed of innumerable tiny colour patches in red, green and blue on the emulsion (20 per millimetre) that functioned like tiny pointillistic filters. Devised around 1925, the *Spicer-Dufay* was actually used in England (named *Dufaycolor*) but only from the beginning of the 30s, during the sound era.

All this and much more was happening while Technicolor was moving towards its definitive, subtractive solution. *Technicolor No. II* started from the idea of simultaneously capturing two identical but mirrored images on the same negative through a *beam-splitter* coded according to a two-coloured filter. From this single negative two relative positives were printed. The gelatin was strengthened through a tanning process and the relief matrices were then dyed orange and blue-green respectively. These two films were finally glued together, becoming the copy for projection (a fragile positive prone to scratching and cupping). The first film, released in 1922, was a semi-fiction documentary entitled *The Toll of the Sea*. The system was subsequently employed for spectacular sequences in some feature films such as *The Ten Commandments* (1923, as an alternative to *Handschiegl*)[118] and *The Uninvited Guest* (1924). This brings us to the fundamental turning point, *Technicolor No. III*: transforming the two positives into print matrices. The process remained similar up until the point where the copies were impressed on the emulsion, though significant changes were made inside the camera, especially regarding

---

116 At least in appearance, the method had a certain simplicity. It then became a printing method for three-dimensional postcards.

117 In principle it recalls the idea that allowed the Lumière brothers to develop the first reversible, coloured and transparent photos: the Autochrome.

118 For details see P. Cherchi Usai, *Le nitrate* ..., cit. p. 102.

the stability of film slippage. Then (analogous to typographical printing), the positives imbibed in cyan and orange were superimposed one at a time on a positive where a slight black impression of the image was printed. Kept perfectly in register by the perforations, the two matrices were transferred by *dye transfer* of the relative colours onto the final copy – initially, they still had one colour on either side. Using this enhancement, dated 1928, Eric von Stroheim shot the sequence of the Corpus Domini procession in *The Wedding March*.

The film studio and shooting

> The film studio is nothing other than a gigantic, very bright photography studio [...]. The best locations [for its construction, *ed.*] are not too far from heavily populated areas with all the resources of modern life, such as easy access to suppliers, transport and the recruitment of staff.[119]

Indeed, Mariani's description can be systematically verified around the world: studios are in locations which may no longer be real suburbs, but only because of the subsequent expansion of urbanisation. After the Dickson-Edison Black Maria, which could be rotated to capture direct sunlight, Méliès' "double" theatre (a stage covered by glass) has long been the prototype for the best possible workplace. Mariani's other specifications "to be able to use the theatre at any time of day and obtain the most varied lighting effects, it will need to be built entirely in glass and iron",[120] hints at how the studio was soon to be totally enclosed. Furthermore, he goes on to specify "Artificial light is the light needed to integrate sunlight on cloudy days and to obtain special lighting effects, such as sun rays, sudden increases in brightness or the simulation of moonlight, etc."[121]

It was a matter of integration, therefore. The widest possible variety of arc lamps (closed globe, Westminster, Regina, Jupiter) but also mercury vapour tubes (initially considered dangerous as they were thought to be radioactive), were mounted side by side in banks. All these lights were compatible with or specific to orthochromatic emulsion. Lights began to be employed during

119 Mariani, *Guida pratica...*, cit., p. 31.

120 Ibidem, p. 33.

121 Ibidem, p. 59.

the early part of the second decade, and in an increasingly systematic manner. Lighting equipment was gradually fine-tuned according to intensity, and it could be suspended or manoeuvred on the ground using stands. This evolution led to the gradual "closure" of the windows, moving towards a design that worked exclusively with artificial light, much like studios today. In 1917, the pioneer of Italian cinema Lamberto Pineschi wrote: "I believe that our installation is the best in Europe, because of its many varied lighting options and its rational arrangement of lamps [...] I obtain such perfect photographic results that I do not regret the absence of sunlight".[122]

And all the filmmakers around the world who became accustomed to interiors and exteriors rebuilt *in the studio*, with increasingly realistic materials, did not regret it either. It became possible to recreate any environment, at any time (day or night ...) or climate (rain, snow ...), relying on lighting systems which could also make use of incandescent bulbs once panchromatic film had been invented. Finally, given the tools to "shape" the scene using light, the person in charge of photographic quality was transformed from a pure technician into a creative participant. Thus, the electricians department was established to manage materials and accessories designed to control lighting. Electricians were also active outdoors using mobile generators to power *lights* that were becoming indispensable for nighttime scenes or to compensate for the absence of sunlight. The *reflection* of natural sunlight could also be redirected using silver-coated panels.[123] Alongside the electricians, a grip crew was created to manoeuvre temporary structures for lights and other accessories (though still primitive) to support the camera even in motion: wheelbarrows, carts, rocker arms and even suspended platforms.

The trick film (also the father of cartoons or animated cinema) the birth of special effects

We have seen how replacement meant interrupting shooting,

122 From "Progresso fotografico" January 1917, quoted in "Immagine, note di storia del cinema", new series n. 4, winter 1986/87, p. 24.

123 Silver but rough, not shiny, to obtain a "diffused" effect: in recent years, however, such heavy and bulky materials have been mostly replaced by sheets of expanded polystyrene.

modifying the necessary details in the frame, and resuming filming. The interruption itself does not affect Cinematic time, but it is effective because the results can be fantastic, unreal, or if necessary even realistic. In the summer of 1896, Georges Méliès noticed this when his rudimentary camera blocked (a modified projector by Robert W. Paul!), he resumed filming a few moments later. When the film was projected[124] an omnibus (a horse-drawn tram) suddenly turned into a hearse (for the first time ever, real time had necessarily and magically been transformed into cinematic time).[125] Méliès immediately adapted this expedient to simplify his stage number *Escamotage d'une dame* in its cinematographic version. He was pointing the way to a new path: illusion as opposed to live footage.

There is only one precedent, *The Execution of Mary Queen of Scots,* made for the Kinetoscope the year before in the USA by the Edison director Alfred Clark. In a few short seconds the film depicts the decapitation of poor Queen Mary (played by Robert Tomae secretary and treasurer of the Kinetoscope Company), after an interruption, the impromptu actor was replaced by a mannequin – most of the extras actually changed posture instead of staying motionless. Whether Méliès had seen it or not is irrelevant:[126] for Clark that trick was quite random, dictated most likely by realism rather than some magic or suggestive effect, indeed there is no hint of any further use of this expedient after this production. For Méliès, instead, it opened a world, it led him to systematically research the opportunities offered by this new medium that had so much in common had with photography.[127]

---

124 After stopping and restarting the camera, the negative of the replacement shot needed to be cleaned – a process of cutting, selecting, eliminating and gluing film clips from different shots. Although this cut-and-paste process initially only concerned images which were very similar (to achieve this fantastic effect the scene and its framing could not be changed) it must be said that it was Méliès who first understood and initiated the practice of creative editing.

125 The film, like two-thirds of Méliès's output, has been lost.

126 It may even have been part of a stock of Kinetoscope films he purchased in England.

127 It is no coincidence that the illusory possibilities of photography appear as a natural evolution of theatrical illusions. In any case, a connection had already been made to cinema according to the most complete printed inventory of "magic", the first edition of which appeared a little more than two years after first Lumière projections: Albert A. Hopkins *Magic: Stage Illusions And Scientific Diversions, Including Trick Photography,* available as an anastatic reprint from 1976 by Dover Publications, Inc.

Photography was already capable of fantastic and even surreal effects, practices inherited from the Phantasmagorias of the Magic Lantern, [128] such double exposures and other technological devices. The camera, initially designed for continuous movement, scrolling endlessly and recording action as long as there was film available, in Méliès' hands was not only stopped, it was used to change the speed[129] and direction[130] to achieve implausible effects which were initially simply defined as tricks. For example visible transformations, apparitions and disappearances accomplished through cross-fading, i.e. progressively closing the diaphragm during a shoot, rewinding and then progressively opening it while filming again over the same raw stock. We have already pointed out that this expedient also functioned thanks to the camera's adjustable shutter, or to a second diaphragm placed in accessory slots in front of the lens. It should be remembered that until the end of the 20s these tricks – soon called *special effects* – were rigorously achieved in-camera, on set, not created a posteriori in the laboratory during development and printing. It was enough to locate the initial frame of each shot in the dark[131] and to protect the scene that had already been filmed by putting a light-proof cap on the lens while rewinding. This facility in moving forwards or backwards by simply turning the crank led to the use of homogeneous backgrounds that were as black as possible, so as not to expose

128 During the 19th century, almost everywhere Magic Lantern shows tended to become *Phantasmagoria*, recalling the late 18th Parisian performances by Étienne-Gaspard Robertson. Through the skilful use of improved magic lanterns, Robertson attempted to pass off esoteric experiences, including ghostly apparitions, as real. Plagiarised by dishonest assistants, Robertson defended himself in court, showing the patent for his *Fantoscope* and other instruments he had developed. Thus, the alleged sorcerer was recast in the role of the great entertainer, paving the way for a "technology of fiction" that is still valid today allowing us to design and construct any situation whether possible or impossible.

129 Accelerating and slowing down, two of the easiest and most incisive expedients used to emphasise action, make them emblematic of the passage of time, but also ironically so (in *Onésime horloger* 1912, by Jean Durand – who also acts in the film – a foolish young man speeds up life incredibly by tampering with the central *clock* so that he can get his inheritance sooner).

130 Reverse motion can be considered cinema's first "special effect", at the early Lumière projections it was used for the reversal of *Demolition of a Wall* (1896) thus reconstructing it virtually. But the "effect" was achieved live, a kind of performance, as in Lantern shows, only using the projector. It was not an in-camera effect. It was therefore a possible option and not a permanent alteration entrusted to the negative: awareness and certainty of "effect" in a film require it to be created during the shooting stage.

131 Making a hole in the film with a device attached to the camera or tying a cotton thread through one of the perforations ... .

the emulsion, allowing for several shots to be taken on adjacent portions of the scenic space. Subsequently cardboard or metal silhouettes (mattes) and additional silhouettes (counter mattes) were added so that the image was composed like a kind of puzzle. Thus doors, windows and other variously shaped objects, or portions of the frame where exposed two or more times to achieve (still referring to Méliès) a multiplication of the same character carrying out different actions (*L'homme orchestre*, 1900), a variation in size between actors (even the visible enlargement of a figure: *Le diable géant*, 1901), and the appearance on the same frame of elements filmed at different times and in different manners, for example, filming horizontally (some beautiful girls dancing) and with the camera suspended vertically (Méliès himself walking up the walls like a fly: *L'homme mouche*,[132] 1902). We have already mentioned the natural use of the matte and counter matte procedure for simulating realistic scenes in the film studio, employed in the USA by Edwin S. Porter in 1902 for the railway ticket office and inside a moving postal wagon in *The Great Train Robbery*.

We have not yet mentioned what is still today the most extraordinary cinematic trick (or effect): applying the substitution principle frame by frame can breathe life into any artificial thing whether it be a drawing, an object or a puppet. And in some languages, such as German, what we call animated film (officially born in France in 1908 with *Fantasmagorie* by Emile Courtet, better known as Cohl) is still today called a *trick film*. This principle of double exposure could also be extended to material which had already been exposed: in the developing bath the part of emulsion that had not been exposed (the black portion) was dissolved and the transparent areas of the negative (not white, as we might call them absentmindedly ...) could be integrated with material from other films, a sort of sandwich that unified elements from different shots on the positive print. Thanks to this technique we had the first interaction between a live character and an animated one:

---

132 The options in positioning the camera in relation to the set are extraordinary, placing it horizontally and then vertically, it is possible to shift between one frame and another editing according to the actors movement, thus seeming to pass smoothly from the floor to what appears to be the wall ... .

Clair de lune Espagnol, dated 1909, again an example of animated film by Emile Cohl (co-director Etienne Armaud). We have not yet said, however, that a decisive development in animation occurred in the United States during the second decade. In an attempt to achieve the most life-like animation possible for human characters, the Austrian brothers Max and Dave Fleischer came up with the idea of filming an actor (in this case Dave dressed as Koko the Clown) against a neutral background, they then projected each frame onto frosted glass on which they placed a sheet of transparent celluloid: the *cel. Cel* had just been discovered[133] to be the ideal material for drawing animation characters, it allowed the setting to be viewed underneath, and it also allowed movements to be broken down keeping some parts fixed and only changing details (such as pupils or lips). Since the opaque pigments[134] (initially just black and white) were applied to the reverse side of the sheet it was possible to obtain a smooth flowing background drawing, so as to simulate every possible movement. In the meantime, to keep the image stable, the various sheets were punched with complementary holes[135] that fitted onto two or more pegs on both the work table and the filming equipment. Tracing a succession of images from real life figures, the Fleischer brothers could give their characters an accurate and analytical reproduction of the phases of movement. But their equipment (patented in 1915 as the *Rotoscope*),[136] with the addition of a camera placed in front of the translucent support surface and equipped with pegs, also allowed them to shoot a projected background, frame by frame (also in movement therefore) and a series of drawings on cel (the coloured pigments covered the other image) layered above the dynamic background. Thus began the endless and hilarious confrontation between the spiteful cartoon clown Koko and his creator Max Fleischer. And with it a systematic mix of reality and artifice that became stabilised and perfected over the

133 Earl Hurd patented *cels* and breakdown in 1914.

134 These materials were considered precious in the early years, when a short film was finished, the cels were washed and reused. Chuck Jones, one of the great American animators, started his career washing *cels* at Ub Iwerks' studio.

135 The *peg system* introduced by Raoul Barré.

136 First film: *Experiment No. 1*, produced by Max and Dave Fleischer for the Bray Pictures Company.

years into a technological process called optical printing, used for animation and much more, and only become obsolete with the arrival of digital technology. It was a process which permitted the creation and management of mobile mattes also obtained from real-life shots by outlining the areas for composite images on *cels*, and, among other things, allowed for the inclusion of writing and titles over the action.

Over time, a variety of other technological expedients were adopted aimed at increasing the evocative quality of the image, especially by enhancing cinematographic space on the actual set. Always in an attempt to achieve the maximum result with minimum effort (of course, in predominantly industrial terms the word minimum has relative value). Specifically:

> *the glass shot*, introduced in 1907 by the American Norman O. Dawn[137] but systematically employed from the 20s (until the advent of digital, it was used extensively, especially in adventure films and monumental historical films). It consisted in setting a large sheet of glass in front of the camera on which an artist had painted part of a landscape or building that completed the physical background. It could be combined with live action thanks to its transparency. Walter G. Hall and Walter Percy Day subsequently perfected the procedure so that artists could create the painting retrospectively, completing what had already been filmed with an in-camera matte;

As far as we know, *rear projection*, or *back projection*, was used for the first time by Norman O. Dawn in 1913.[138] It consisted in the rear-projection of a landscape sequence, not necessarily in motion, on a translucent screen in front of which the actors perform; it was completed with a few real items of scenery (trees, rocks, interiors of cars, boats, planes, etc.). The camera in front of the scene shot the action in the studio combined with this life-like background. The shutters of both camera and projector needed to be synchronised. This procedure, which became very popular from the 1930s, declined in quality with the advent of colour cinema, in particular due to the poor sensitivity of the first available emulsions;

137 First film: *Missions of California*.

138 First film: *The Drifter*.

the *Schüfftan process* developed from 1923 by the great German cinematographer Eugen Schüfftan for Fritz Lang (*Die Nibelungen*). This process connected a real shot to a scale model[139] (but also to photographs or paintings) through a mirror placed at a 45° angle to the camera: the mirror reflected the model which was positioned in such a way that it completed an overall image obtained by scratching off the silver surface in the area that framed the real situations or stage set used in real scale.

But setting actors into anomalous, eccentric, dangerous or fantastic situations was to become one of the increasingly pressing requirements in the developing area of special effects. In order to do this, it was necessary to transform the human body into a matte and, what is more, a moving one. In the late 20s C. Dodge Dunning managed to create a process for mobile mattes working exclusively with black and white negatives – it was later perfected by Roy Pomeroy – it became known as the *Dunning process*. It was very complex: substantially it was necessary to shoot two distinct films in the studio (before a homogeneously illuminated screen exploiting the difference in light sensitivity between orthochromatic and panchromatic emulsions), one with the silhouettes (or matte) of the action and the other with the complementary (counter matte). Starting from these materials, through a series of steps using an optical printer in the printing laboratory (a combination of a projector and a camera), it became possible to pierce a third shot filmed under whatever circumstances with the overall dimensions of the moving body, inserting the detail previously filmed into a final composite negative.

Developing and printing

From the outset of "animated photography" (1889) William Laurie Dickson had prepared a development system and a continuous contact printing system, at the Edison laboratories. So as to be exposed and fixed, both negative and positive were wound on a wooden drum that was then half-submerged in flat, shallow tanks containing chemical compounds. Turning on its axis, the drum progressively dipped the film in the baths and gradually completed the operation which could be controlled under red light (the film

---

139 Three-dimensional models or *miniatures* are an integral part of the illusions that can be achieved through careful use of the focal length of certain lenses as well as relative depth of field.

90

was orthochromatic). For printing instead, a continuous printer with an electric motor dragged the negative superimposed on raw stock across a large drum illuminated by an electric lamp of variable intensity. In 1897 (when the Cinematograph was put on sale), the more pragmatic Lumière brothers – whose experience dated from the very beginning – advised the use of buckets with a capacity of a dozen litres for development, washing and fixing. For printing, instead, they had a double-axle cartridge, one axle for the negative and the other for the raw stock: turning the crank the two films were dragged by the claw and paired, gelatin against gelatin.[140] It was necessary, once the lens had been removed, to position oneself, at a suitable distance, in front of a light source such as a gas or oil lamp, a white wall, or later an electric light bulb. Turning the crank at a greater or lesser speed could compensate for exposure errors by increasing or decreasing the amount of light that would pass through the negative. In England, in 1895, Robert W. Paul copied Edison films for the Kinetoscope (not covered by copyright in Europe), using a manual printer that effected a simultaneous passage of negative and raw stock in front of a gas jet in a darkroom. The film was developed by attaching it with spacing pegs to frames which were then immersed and shaken in deep wooden troughs. At first, the film hung out to dry, but later he preferred to enclose it in ever larger wooden drums. These more or less rudimentary systems were sufficient for materials which, we should remember, did not exceed 50 feet and were treated in-house by producers who probably conceived and guarded their processing secrets. In his memoirs, Méliès explained how he had adopted wooden drums for the development process. Among other things, they could be transported and re-installed in various stations where the chemical baths needed to complete the process were located. During these steps it was possible to observe the images developing, under red light, so as to compensate or even customise the final result, if necessary, varying the immersion time in the various acids. In those years, the growing popularity of illustrated photo-postcards made it

---

140 Contrary to what happened during filming, in projection the emulsion is not placed facing the lens.

necessary to automate the manufacturing process. Thus, in early 1895, the first machines were introduced in America which transported the exposed paper through the various baths before being *rewound* in a sort of gas stove where they were dried. The first to patent such a device was Cecil Hepworth in England in 1898: a gas engine drove toothed rollers which engaged the perforations so that the film flowed regularly through a succession of troughs.

For colouring, the systems underwent a similar evolutionary process starting from simple procedures (buckets or frames) and gradually introducing, from the second decade of the 20th century, machines with *tubes* in which the film was gently guided by rubber rollers or sprockets. Zigzagging out of and in to cylindrical containers immersed in coloured liquids or various reactants for tinting or mordent toning, the film finally reached glass cabinets in which it was dried with hot air. Employing this principle, perfected between 1912 (Gaumont) and 1914 (Pathé) with the creation of units that defined the various stages of the process (developing, washing, fixing, washing, and drying), the first continuous processors became available. This was precisely the time when the narrative in cinema was growing, reaching the dimension of the *feature film*. Other issues were then tackled: diversified development depending on the quality of the negative or temperature control, in particular of the development bath, which was controllable visually and remained directly proportional to the speed of the film. The arrival of panchromatic emulsion, which had to be treated in complete darkness, made it necessary to automate the various steps and led, consequently, to a more scientific approach to all the phases of the process.

As we said, analogous systems were developed for colouring. The negatives were thus assembled in homogeneous rolls, not connected to any narrative logic, but according to the type and quality of colouring that that group of scenes required. This created the need for an additional department that had to compose the positives for projection, and which also had to add, as we shall see, titles and captions.

Meanwhile, printing also underwent continuous improvements: an initial subdivision remained between continuous printers that superimposed negative and positive and intermittent printers that advanced frame by frame thanks to an alternating mechanism. The latter was the preferred system in Europe (the leading figure being the Frenchman André Debrie who constantly perfected his patents between 1907 and 1920), giving particular care to the alignment of perforations for optimal control in setting up copies. In America, however, thanks to Bell & Howell, a continuous printer became available as of 1916 which has, in principle, remained virtually unchanged. In both cases the fundamental element that required development was the quantity of printing light which had to be adjusted as quickly as possible, scene by scene, so as to correct errors or to compensate for differences in the sensitivity of the negative used. This problem was also gradually solved, and eventually became both automatic and replicable after careful analysis of the original negative. Needless to say, constructively speaking, over time the continuous printing machine generated a lot of work. These improvements coincided with the birth of independent industrial units for this type of processing, relieving producers of the burden of carrying out such operations.

To complete the work, there was a department that took care of the titles, intertitles or captions. The films were initially presented without any specific notification[141] except as in the case of Edison, writings on some frames that sought to define *copyright* in the absence of legislation. For the same reason, such writings then passed from the film itself (a dry stamp impressed at the beginning or the end of the film) to the actual scenery of the film: placards were placed in a great variety of places, showing the producer's name or logo and for a time their names or logos even ended up imprinted on the edge of copies outside the perforations. Titling began more or less at the same time, in addition to using original graphics that combined the company name in a symbol or in letters. Then, when intertitles began to be set between the various scenes, not only were they almost always personalised and numbered progressively, they were often given a chronological number attributed to that particular film by the producer. With the birth

141 In the very early days, street vendors would only advertise the *system*, proudly calling out the brand of the equipment in use: Edison, Lumière and so on.

of the *feature film*, when at least the names of directors and actors finally began to appear on screen, some of the *title cards* were enriched with friezes or original drawings – however, not those with dialogues. Alfred Hitchcock entered the world of cinema in the 20s as a title-card designer. These were painted or composed with movable characters or even printed in a small in-house typography on cards (hence the most correct term used to identify them) and then filmed by suspending a camera perpendicularly above them (in Italy a similar device used to make cartoons was generically called a *titler*); or, after a similar composition process, printed as photographs that were filmed by coupling a camera with a sort of magic lantern. On the negative, their position was indicated in a variety of ways: inserting no more than three frames with the text (flash titles); using a large X on two or three frames linked to progressive numbers; a directly transcription or at least the beginning of the sentence in the same space.

Assembly gave the film its definitive form, a film draft was used to identify the succession of scenes and relative title cards; all the necessary pieces were patiently put in sequence and glued together. For the foreign market, the intertitles were translated and filmed and set in their identifiable positions on the film, according to the original draft.

Ultimately, since they were made up of many pieces of celluloid glued together, the positive copies were very fragile.

Projection

Retracing the main steps of invention, we have already discussed aspects of both reversible and diversified devices (cameras, printers, projectors), as well as the various principles of intermittent motion, from the claw, to the eccentric cam, and ultimately the Maltese cross. Likewise, we have already mentioned *flicker*, an annoying light pulsation on the screen, due to imperfections in the shutter. And though we must not forget *La Grille,* a black paper fan with a series of tiny holes supplied at Gaumont projections up to around 1907: "an ingenious device for the purpose of suppressing any trepidation or glow in projections; [...] Waving this fan in front of the eyes [...] allowed the scene to be viewed in absolute "steadiness",[142] one of the main issues in early projections was the actual production of light. At the turn of the century, the long history of the Magic Lantern had left a legacy of methodologies and materials: the very dangerous *oxyetheric lamp* (oxygen and ether), the *Oxyhydrogen* lamp (oxygen and hydrogen) and the *limelight* (oxygen and alcohol). But, as we know from Edison's experiments, cinema evolved alongside electricity, and if an electric motor was soon to set the equipment in motion, it was the carbon arc lamp that became a stable fixture inside the (no longer magic) lantern and a fundamental component of the cinema projector. As in the camera, the mechanical part was completed with a pair of drive sprockets which guided the perforated film before and after the projection aperture below which the intermittent device was located. Over the years, the positive copy was to take on ever greater importance. Since it was almost never[143] sold in a form ready for projection, a series of accessories was soon invented. There were gluing machines, essential both for repairing broken films and gluing *reels* together – at their longest reels were 1000 feet (305 meters) long. There were reels (or *spools*) of varying sizes on which the film was wound, after first being transferred to a variant that could be opened on one side (*the split reel*), turning the crank of a rewind device allowed the whole film to be loaded. This description of earlier systems explains why various other systems/tools were introduced and have remained in use with some modifications and automations. Devices were soon added (to interrupt the flow of light and protect and isolate the film) to limit the damage caused by inevitable celluloid fires. There was an important refinement whereby the maltese cross could be shifted vertically to adjust the frame regardless of how it was printed in relation to the perforations. This meant that the annoying phenomenon of *misframing* could be solved without having to shift the matte which would require a much taller screen.

Each country gradually established legal regulations for the custody and handling of these flammable materials as well as the location of the projection booth (which, if not actually non-existent, was initially a temporary structure); in the first stable cinemas it was

142 G. Re, *Il cinematografo...*, cit. p. 82.

143 If not just as an option, but very few distributors accepted it and only as of the 80s.

given its own entrance outside the auditorium. Projection speed could be varied using a rheostat, adapting the speed (from 16 f/s upward) to the circumstances or, better, to the music which, as of 1908,[144] could also be either freshly composed or an adaptation of pre-existing themes used for a given film.

For years alternative intermittent systems were sought, but a completely convincing solution was never found. For example, in 1922 the Venetian engineer Luigi Selvatico patented a continuous motion projector based on a rotating prism, using Reynaud's *optical compensation*. But he was not the only one, and if some devices with similar principles were even produced commercially, it was the Maltese cross that continued to make audience's dreams come true.

144 The first composer to write an original film score was Camille Saint Saëns who wrote music for *L'assassinat du Duc de Guise* made by the company of the Comédie Française, both in front of and behind the camera. It was a marketing operation aimed at legitimising, once and for all, the artistic stature of cinema, which many considered to be no better than a circus act.

Chapter Thirteen

Cinema Talks

Sound

> To merit the epithet animated projection, cinema still lacked an obvious aspect inherent in our expectations of living reality. [...] A crash of thunder could be imitated very well using a thin sheet of metal [...] [145]

In 1909, Liesegang noted how theatres continuously developed and perfected instruments for the production of noises. Thus, a "live" performance could be given at each screening, alongside or in alternative to the music (the main accompaniment). Other accounts, from almost everywhere in the world, tell of attempts to give voice to the characters by using actors in the hall, or even better, behind the screen. Such operations foreshadow a whole range of different contributions that are generally grouped today under the term *post-production*.[146] However, such performances were not what cinema required in its day to day routine, especially when we consider that from its inception the objective had been to couple image with sound that was already coded and reproduced through some form of technology. While the phonograph (on cylinders) and even better it immediate successor the gramophone (on shellac disc) was a parallel yet unsatisfactory path that evolved alongside cinema in its first thirty years, other principles ultimately allowed cinema to speak.

The first, in essence, was based on light: a pulsating light, derived from the modulations of sound picked up by a microphone and transformed into an electric current that activated a light bulb: projecting this pulsation onto a film in continuous motion, it

145 F.P. Liesegang, *Il cinematografo...*, cit., pp. 313–316.

146 This term comes from television and includes *editing*, *titling*, *special optical* and *sound effects* (noises), *dubbing*, *mixing*, *editing*, etc. Today, these specialised and logistically separate interventions, thanks to TV technology increasingly integrated with computers, can be accomplished, albeit progressively, in a single multi-purpose location.

recorded variations of intensity and transparency. This visual coding of sound, crossed by a constant light, transferred the variations of intensity and transparency to a photoelectric cell[147] which was, in turn, able to bring the pulse back to a modulated electric current. Inspired by other experiments with different objectives, the German physicist Ernst Rühmer created the first *optical column* in 1901, however, he did not bring this concept much further. It was Eugène Lauste, a Frenchman operating between America and England, who took up the challenge. In 1906, he was granted a patent for a technique that envisaged the direct transcription of image and sound onto a film where the available space was divided equally between the two. The method used to obtain this "code" was being perfected, yet it was still far from any possible exploitation, especially because diode and triode valves were just being developed at that time. These were the first *thermionic valves* which would eventually make it possible to manage and amplify an electrical signal making it audible to large audiences in spacious environments. The first results were achieved almost simultaneously in Europe and America. In Germany, Josef Engl, Joseph Massolle and Hans Vogt formed the Tri-Ergon Company in 1918 which developed an original technology that was officially presented towards the end of 1922. Meanwhile, in the USA, Lee de Forest, the inventor of the triode, had been at work on the development of speaking cinema since 1919. He perfected his *Phonofilm* between 1921 and 1924 (with other researchers, primarily Theodore W. Case) which, though it did work, was not completely convincing. It was Case alone instead, who fine-tuned the last details, both electronically and mechanically, convincing the Fox Film Corporation to purchase the system in 1926 under the name *Movietone*. What we simplistically define as details were the optimal miniaturisation of the light code so that it occupied a relative space (certainly not half as envisaged by Lauste) on the 35mm surface; the other fundamental element, the photocell, in turn, was made with different materials for an ever more precise

---

147 The rare element selenium produces differences in current when struck by light. This property was described in America in 1873, and the subsequent invention, the "photocell", was refined and led the way to numerous inventions such as the television, the telephone and sound in cinema, as well as more banal items like safety control in elevator doors.

decoding of the light pulses. Furthermore, there were mechanical problems in maintaining a constant speed: once it had left the intermittent element, the film had to resume continuous motion so that the *soundtrack* could be read correctly at a distance of twenty-one frames. To produce acceptable sound, shooting and projection were definitively set at 24 f/s.[148]

But the key element of the whole process was amplification, developed by Western Electric from 1913 onwards, so that in collaboration with the other devices mentioned above, sound finally became a reality in cinemas in 1926. In actual fact, as we have already mentioned, right through the *silent period*, more or less functional systems proposed what came to be known as *Phonoscènes*: songs, operatic arias and monologues with exceptional performers (e.g. Sarah Bernhardt and Enrico Caruso), either as once off events or in specialised environments. They were filmed in rigorously fixed shots and the sound was recorded on disks. Time and time again, spectators were enticed by announcements about the quality of a given patent: finally the combination of electricity and mechanics would achieve perfect synchronisation between the two separate sources (image and sound). Gaumont was also at the forefront in this research which, starting in 1900, materialised in 1910 as *Elgéphone*.[149] Thanks to an ingenious compressed air amplification system this device could propagate sound in the immense hall of the Gaumont-Palace (it was even coupled, a couple of years later, with their *Chronochrome*). But the absolute "first time" occurred in America, with the *Vitaphone*, developed by Western and Bell (the same Bell as the telephone) which, after about a year of experimentation with dozens of shorts, on 6 August 1926 managed to replace the orchestra (or organ, even one that simulated noises[150]) with large discs (over 40 cm wide) that turned at 33 1/3 rpm, each coupled to a celluloid reel

148 Over the years indeed, projection speed, which even had different frequencies within the same film, was progressively stabilising at around 24 f/s, though for the most diverse reasons, as Kevin Brownlow writes in *Film muti. Quale era la velocità giusta?* , in "Griffithiana" 26–27, September 1986, p. 70.

149 "Elgé as L and G", or Léon Gaumont ...

150 In English speaking countries, in particular, extravagantly decorated cinemas included powerful organs as part of their fixed equipment to which a similar apparatus had been coupled to produce live sound effects.

(a classic 300 meters). While the first film, *Don Juan*, was a huge success, the following year the second film *The Jazz Singer* (directed by the same director: Alan Crosland) impressed the audience even more, it was a melodrama in which the singer and actor Al Jolson apparently both sang and spoke ... Thus cinema with sound and speech began, there was initial resistance from many filmmakers who continued to believe in the universality of body language.

Soon *Movietone* and other similar systems (all compatible despite the fact that the similarities triggered years of economic and legal controversy) gained the upper hand, and not only because of easier management. This led to a rapid development in specific equipment (*booms* to support the microphones, *records* for optical recording, the *mixers* to mix the various sound sources: words, music and noises) as well as subsequent, continuous improvements. New forms of encoding were also developed that improved the precision, from the initial *variable density* (modulation represented in greater or less opacity) to *variable area* (an effective graphic representation of segments that are more or less acute and frequent).

The camera

In the early 1920s, small cameras[151] with reduced autonomy came on the market equipped with a clockwork mechanism (twenty-five meters of film in metal magazines that were easily replaced even in daylight). Then a little later, to facilitate movement in the studio, lighter cameras driven by an electric motor came into use. With the advent of sound, the electric motor became indispensable to keep constant speed. However, this made it essential to close the camera in a glass box to reduce noise, thus blocking mobility once again. Then came the *blimp*, a heavy and bulky sound-absorbing casing around the camera, which, nevertheless, gave the equipment back its manageability. As of the 30s, mobility was increasingly facilitated with specific devices, such as panoramic heads on tripods, which gradually became smoother, dollies on rubber wheels that ran on modular tracks in natural exteriors and even levers that moved the camera like a crane. Over time, all

151 Such as the Dresden-based ICA's Kinamo equipped with a Zeiss lens, designed in 1922 and available, in the *spring-driven* version, as of 1924.

this equipment would undergo continuous and incessant practical improvements that tended to combine strength and lightness, thanks to the materials employed.

The mattes in the camera and, obviously, the projector's aperture gates shrank to one side – shifting the centre of the image towards the inside – to accommodate the soundtrack (between the two and three millimeters). The image in the first "talkies" was virtually "squared"; to restore the traditional 4/3 ratio, they soon brought the interline between frames into line with the width of the sound column, imperceptibly adjusting the proportion between height and base to 1:1.37. In America, among the cameras being developed to cater for these new needs, the Mitchell NC stood out, it was silent and moreover, was equipped with a framing control system that permitted direct vision through the lens while frame testing. The entire mechanical drive could be shifted laterally and then correctly repositioned during actual shooting, i.e. when the cameraman observed the action in an external Galilean viewfinder with approximate parallax correction. Some European manufacturers ensured the control of framing either with prism systems or through an eyepiece that allowed one to see the frame through the actual negative.[152] While, thanks to German industry, the Nazi propaganda machine, which sought popular consensus principally through cinema, availed of an authentic jewel: a light, portable camera that enabled continuous vision during shooting. In the Arriflex (by designers-manufacturers Arnold & Richter) the shutter was set at 45° to the surface facing the lens and it mirrored the light in such a way as to intercept it and send it to the viewfinder via a prism, even when in motion. Relatively light, equipped with interchangeable magazines and a three lens turret, it was extremely functional (the body of the motor was also a handle). As of 1936 the *Arri* documented the pomp and evils of the Nazi regime. Once the patent expired after the war, all new cameras adopted this *reflex* principle. Despite its loud noise,[153] the Arriflex long remained the most commonly used camera, in

---

152 A system that remained in use, in black and white, until the 1950s.

153 In the final scene of Carlo Lizzani's *The Verona Process* the sound made by the *Arri* while filming the bodies of those executed by firing squad seems to reiterate the idea of shooting.

Italy in particular where *live sound recording* continued to be avoided for years. In 1934, a further refinement by Mitchell finally managed to make an electrical connection with the sound recording system, thus maintaining synchronisation between the two codes (handled separately for all stages of processing up to the so-called *sample print*); over time this became universally indispensable (it was the definitive *Blimped* Newsreel Camera or BNC). This connection, however, has no longer been necessary for at least twenty years, since the introduction of quartz controls in electric motors which ensure constant speed. As for lenses, beyond the intrinsic evolution in definition and brightness, thanks to the use of ever more refined crystals and design that have been entrusted to computers for years now, the only significant novelty dates back to the end of the 50s. In truth, the Zoom lens had already been used in photography since the end of the 1800s and was also employed in cinematography, as of the 1930s, especially as a projection lens. With improvements in design it became possible to maintain focus while changing different focal lengths, and though it was used occasionally in productions[154] between the 30s and 40s, it became part of the repertoire of camera accessories in the 50s; among its most convinced supporters in Italy was Roberto Rossellini, starting from *Era notte a Roma* (*Escape by Night*) (1960). The greatest achievement in terms of brightness in non-variable lenses was attained by Stanley Kubrick who adopted a Zeiss lens described as "brighter than the human eye" (f: 0.95) to film *Barry Lyndon* in almost exclusively in natural sources of light (daylight, candles etc. not without some transgressive but perceptible reinforcement) evoking 18th century English painting.

The latest cine camera models, which are becoming lighter, quieter and more ergonomic (like the Austrian Moviecam), allow the film to be transformed into a video signal on a small monitor. A monitor has turned out to be essential in using the *steadicam* (invented by Garrett Brown) which, thanks to an iso-elastic arm has given the camera total mobility since 1975; likewise the crane, introduced the following year, which supports a remote-controlled camera moved with a mobile telescopic arm set on a trolley.

---

154 In Italy too: for example, in *Scipione l'Africano* (1937) by Carmine Gallone.

Colour

From the 30s to the 50s, other systems attempted to reproduce *natural colours* in cinema. Toning, imbibition and other methods became obsolete as sound progressed since transparency was required to correctly read the optical column on the positive; but that was not the principal reason.

In accordance with the principle of additive colour, attempts were made, with multiple lenses, to have the same frame not in two but three (even four!) small images with the basic colour codes. Among the logos that engaged with this complex experimentation, Bassani, Francita and Ruxcolor just about managed to reach public screenings. However it was the *two-colour* systems using the *subtractive* principle that established themselves, as they were relatively easier to manage. *Duplitized* positives continued to be produced, obtained, for example, from filming with similar negatives, or, alternatively, from two negatives that flowed together, in contact, behind the film gate (*bipack*). This latter was the element that was introduced in the fourth and final *Technicolor* system and finally managed to obtain a real tricolour system. Behind the lens, a prism with a built-in filter separated the light emissions.[155] The green light impresses a first film strip, an orthochromatic negative, while the blues and reds were diverted 90° towards another gate behind which two other negatives flowed, the red on the first and the blue on the second. In printing, the *dye transfer* was thus enriched with a third element, definitively producing the three complementary colours needed to reproduce the entire spectrum (cyan, magenta and yellow). After years of experimentation it was initially given in an exclusive contract to Disney and the milestones of the *Technicolor tripack* can be summarised between 1932 and 1934 as follows: 1932, the first production, part of the *Silly Symphony* series, entitled *Flower and Trees*; 1934, *La Cucharacha*,[156] a first short with real characters but shot completely in studio; 1935, *Becky Sharp*,[157] the first full-length feature film ever shot

155 An identical system continues to be used in television cameras which were initially equipped with three cathode tubes and then, in portable devices, with three CCDs.

156 By Lloyd Corrigan with Paul Porcasi, Steffi Duna and Don Alvarado.

157 By Rouben Mamoulian with Miriam Hopkins, Frances Dee and Cedric Hardwicke, an RKO production.

entirely in studio under artificial light; 1937, *The Trail of the Lonesome Pine*,[158] the first film that included external shots. The delicate but heavy Mitchell camera (the magazines contained 300 meters) adapted to this system was monumental in appearance, especially since it was housed inside a large blimp to keep it silent. Up until the mid-1950s, as long as the system remained in use, shooting in *Technicolor tripack* meant using only *Technicolor* equipment, employees, and following their binding technological advice.[159]

But if *Technicolor* remained the first and for a long time the best system of *natural colours* designed for homogeneous and persistently high quality copies,[160] its complexity and expense probably accelerated the race towards a technology that would unify the chromatic information on the negative rather than the positive. Technology had been developing simultaneously in photography: starting from the chromatic sensitisation of silver bromide gelatin, accomplished by H.W. Vogel in 1873, and chromogenic development technique in 1909 by the chemists Homolka and Fischer. A purely chemical problem, therefore, had been perfected over the years and found its first application in cinema in the early 30s. The first system incorporating three layers of sensitive colours into an emulsion on the same film was patented by the Hungarian chemist, Bela Gaspar, in 1933. In actual fact, *Gasparcolor* circumvented the obstacle in filming using three black and white negatives, (or three shots on the same negative, with the relative filters, for animation),[161] and in printing, with positive emulsion on both sides of the film (one with one layer and the other with two superimposed layers) which required very complex development procedures but resulted in extraordinary, stable colours over time. Likewise,

---

158 By Henry Hathaway with Henry Fonda, Fred MacMurray, Sylvia Sidney, a Paramount production.

159 The antagonism between the English headquarters of Technicolor and G.R. Aldo (Aldo Graziati) during the making of Luchino Visconti's *Senso* (1954) was famous. Who knows what other results would have been achieved had Aldo not passed away half way through the project.

160 The durability of this colour was also much less evanescent than the *chemical colour* we are about to discuss.

161 It was precisely in the field of animated films and advertising in particular that Gasparcolor *continued* to be used up until the 1950s (it was printed in England).

Kodachrome, marketed in a 16mm amateur format as of 1935, is one of the systems least subject to colour deterioration because dyes (couplers) were inserted during development to replace the black and white that had been encoded in layers sensitive to the three colours during shooting. The extreme complexity of the processes made it essential that all operations be carried out at the "parent company". However, *Kodachrome* (still in use today, especially in photography) had a big limit, cinematically speaking: it was a reversal film and therefore produced only the original. But, given the excellent quality of the final product, between the 40s and the 50s, Technicolor developed a method to produce three matrices for serial printing from those *positive monopacks*. In Europe, Agfa had also undertaken a similar path. Indeed, the studies that led to *Kodachrome* were, in part, actually based on the insights of Wilhelm Schneider a researcher at the German firm. The Agfacolor Neu, again 16mm and a reversal film, became a reality the following year, in 1936. However, in Germany, they decide to go a step further, finally creating the first negative-positive colour *monopack* system in 1939. It was tested with a short film *Ein Lied verklingt*, shot in 1938 and presented in 1939, the same year in which *Frauen sind doch bessere Diplomaten*, the first feature film was made. While the war delayed its diffusion, it did not prevent its development: in the 40s the negative was diversified into film for natural light and artificial light, while maintaining a rather low sensitivity (10 DIN, equivalent to 8 ASA). Meanwhile, the propaganda machine was in motion, and it was Goebbels in person who entrusts Veit Harlan, a director close to the regime, with the task of exalting this German discovery. With this refined and more sensitive emulsion, in Prague in 1942, Harlan filmed *Die goldene Stadt* which was previewed in the last self-sufficient edition of the Venice Film Festival (a festival that had been, since its birth in 1932, a timely witness of the development of various colour systems). When the Soviets occupied the industrial zone of Berlin the procedure was quickly acquired and became *Sovcolor* which afforded Sergei Eisenstein yet another, though unrepeatable, practical application of his theories, in this case regarding colour, in the "banquet" sequence in his *Ivan the Terrible Part 2* made between 1945 and 1946 (but released by Stalin, only in 1958 and distributed in Italy in 1960 with the title *La congiura dei Boiardi [The Conspiracy of the Boyars]*). At the end of the war, the Agfacolor patent (together with others developed during the Nazi regime) was made public, and became the basis of many other *monopack* systems which appeared on the international market with slight modifications and further improvements. The American *Anscocolor* (1945), for example, was derived directly from the German original since the factory was actually Agfa's US branch before the war. There was the Belgian *Gevacolor* (1948) and the Italian *Ferraniacolor* (1949: though the basis of this process dated back to 1941). Kodak, however, always attentive to the many varied patents being developed, providing appropriate materials on a case-by-case basis, delayed its entry into the *negative-positive monopack* market. It did not happen until 1951, when *masking* was applied to the manufacture of film, a refinement they had adopted in 1948 for a new photographic negative called *Ektacolor*. Thanks to the quality of this new product and Kodak's undoubted industrial and promotional strength, the introduction of *Eastman-color* marked a point of no return. Not only did Technicolor gradually abandon the three-negative camera, keeping the imbibing system only for printing (until 1975), but the major film producers adopted the procedure (which, from the outset, obviously also included the positive film) customising it under various names such as *Warnercolor, De Luxe Color, Metrocolor,* etc. In 1955, the Japanese *Fujicolor* came on the scene, the only true and reliable antagonist that continues to contend with the Kodak to this day (it started to penetrate the American market in 1967). And if the alternative market almost exclusively concerns itself with printing positives for screenings, further developments which still continue involve more and more sensitive emulsions to obtain ever increasing definition. In the production system this means less need to reinforce natural light and therefore, consequently, greater processing speed; less loss of time positioning the lighting equipment with a consequent reduction of personnel in lighting team: as usual the maximum result with the minimum effort.

The film studio and filming

The advent of sound created the only real revolution in the history of film, and as it brought about changes in the cinema theatres, it did the same in the studios. These spaces which by this time had become completely covered and totally manageable with artificial light, needed to be transformed according to precise acoustic criteria. The bulk and weight of sound recording equipment and its limited fidelity made it advisable to avoid outdoor filming as much as possible, particularly in urban environments. Therefore, studios began to equip their nearby open spaces with sets of sidewalks, streets, squares, crossroads and pools for maritime environments and more besides, adapted from one production to the next when the available resources could not afford brand new designs and constructions. Thus, starting from the 1930s, there was an increasingly urgent need for simple *special effects to enrich* the lifelike quality, but also the spectacularity, of images created for convenience or due to technical and practical difficulties, in the comfort of ever better equipped and more efficient *studios*. It was thanks to the technological refinement of the shooting equipment (stands, trolleys, dollies), of lighting (with the gradual elimination of incandescent lights in favour of halogen lamps first in the 70s, and then *Gas-discharge lamps* in the 80s) and, finally, of sound recording systems (entrusted, as we will see shortly, to magnetic recording) which, as we have said, became increasingly manageable and lightweight, together with ever more sensitive emulsions that yielded images which no longer deteriorated in definition, that allowed cinema, to abandon the studio. Consequently, any ambiance or corner, external or internal, in any part of the world could unconditionally become a film set.

Film

Despite the fact that technology was not up to the task, in 1911 in England there were those who were thinking of stereophonic sound in cinema, engaging a separate film synchronised with the images. This hypothesis found its first practical application in 1931, using a similar two-track optical system, in special projections of the film *Hell's Angels*,[162] which recreated some amazing air battles from the First World War. Experimentation continued during the 30s with music transcribed onto several optical columns on film. It must have lent extraordinary added value to *Fantasia*, the animated music feature that Disney planned for cinema by cinema screening in 1940 with an even more powerful system (eight audio channels) developed with RCA and called *Fantasound*. The sheer complexity of its installation and management was just one of the variables that decreed the initial flop of what has since become a definitive cult movie. After that, the idea of stereophonic sound had to wait until the 1950s and for a new technology based on an intuition with which the Edison laboratories had not even experimented in 1885: recording sound by changing the magnetic state of a metal support. It was the Danish engineer Valdemar Poulsen who applied it, as of 1898, magnetising a thin steel wire and presenting his Phonograph, a reversible machine for recording and playing, at the 1900 Paris Exposition. Poulsen then discovered that it was possible to cancel the recording and reuse the support again. Though steel wire continued to be employed in equipment built in Europe and elsewhere until the 50s, in Germany in the late 20s paper was used first and then cellulose acetate covered with iron oxide. And if the BBC already had a tape recorder in 1932 called the *Blattnerphone,* it was again in Germany that AEG, in collaboration with I.G.Farben, marketed the magnetophone in 1935. As happened with the *Arri reflex* and *Agfacolor*, the details of this invention also became public domain at the end of the war. This led to the rapid development of other equipment in the United States. We have already spoken – in the earlier chapter dedicated to film – of those large formats that appeared between 1929 and 1930 which were soon forgotten. Twenty years later, in reaction to the growing success of TV, the American film industry developed super-spectacular systems in an attempt to bring spectators back to the cinemas. The first invention was *Cinerama*[163] which used three synchronised 35mm devices, both

162 Produced and directed by the billionaire Howard Hughes. It cost a fortune since it was shot a second time because of the addition of sound.

163 In actual fact, the idea of multiple synchronised films and projections, even on cylindrical surfaces has, as usual, earlier precedents in the history of the Magic Lantern (Chase's *Cyclorama*, in America, in 1895) and then in cinema (Grimoin-Sanson's *Cinéorama*, although announced for the 1900 Paris exposition, could not go ahead for security reasons).

for shooting and projection, with coincident shooting-projection axes, and a screen curved 145° horizontally and 55° vertically. Designed in 1948, it was presented in New York on September 30, 1952. The sound was magnetic and recorded on seven separate tracks on a fourth 35mm film, perforated to ensure the perfect synchronisation of all the components. This complex technology that required, among other things, dedicated locations (the *Cinerama* installations around the world totalled 41) did not last more than ten years. However, beyond the artfully engaging documentaries with their exasperated perspectives (lifelike rides on airplanes, roller coasters and so on), two feature films were made in 1962: *How the West was Won*, with famous stars and directors, and above all, extraordinary natural settings, and the magical *The Wonderful World of the Brothers Grimm*. And while *Cinerama* would have to change in order to survive, in the meantime Fox, having taken Chrétien's hypergonar out of the drawer, presented its revolutionary *Cinemascope*[164] in 1953. Revolutionary above all because it led to the definitive layout of cinemas, broadening the screen as well as the range and quality of sounds and noises. Indeed, in its original concept *Cinemascope* had a ratio of 1:2.55, taking back width from the optical column and making room for 4 tracks of ferrous oxide by narrowing the perforations. In this case, a multi-track playback head positioned behind the projection aperture, yielded stereo sound with three sources behind the screen and one in the hall. Thus magnetic recording came to be included on copies intended for distribution. Despite a certain fragility, it was to remain the only means of improving sound quality for a long time. At least until the masterly inventions of engineer Ray Dolby.

As of the early 50s, all the phases of sound, from the live recording of voices and music, to the various phases of editing and mixing, shifted optical to magnetic, a support which, moreover, did not require development and was even reusable. This is also because in 1950, in Switzerland, the Polish engineer Stefan Kudelski had built the prototype of the NAGRA, a portable audio recorder

---

164 The first film was *The Robe* by Harry Koster.

(with *spring* motor) with a 1/4 inch tape that was soon to become and still remains the symbol of *direct* sound recording in cinema.

For cinemas that wished to just improve up their projection equipment, *scope* became compatible thanks to the printing of monophonic versions with a normal optical column. Returning to its usual position, the optical column eliminated a small portion of the image slightly reducing the overall width (1:2.35). Also in 1953, Paramount adopted its own spectacular system, employing magnetic stereo with the film running horizontally instead of vertically, thus occupying almost double the negative surface (as had already been the case, since 1924, for the *Leica*[165] camera format). By engaging eight instead of four perforations, on the screen *VistaVision*[166] yielded an aspect ratio of 1:1.85. In this case the equipment for projection would have to undergo an even more radical transformation. Thus, the negative rectangle began to be optically reduced and inserted, in print, into the normal positive position in which the more elongated relationship could be preserved. On the copies the frame line was thicker and, during projection, it was cut by an aperture mask, while the image was enlarged using shorter focal length lenses reaching the screen in a width just halfway between *normal* and *scope*. Because of the increasingly higher quality of emulsions, in less than a decade shooting in *VistaVision* was dropped. Nevertheless, the system remained in use until the *digital* era in units that processed material for *special effects*: the large format and the need for optical reduction in the final phases made the indispensable artifices of some special effects less obvious.

While the rectangular format was also spreading in Europe under the generic name of wide-screen, it was managed directly during filming by simply adopting the appropriate aperture mask (the European version was less squeezed with an aspect ratio of 1.1:66). Such masks were sometimes not even put in place during takes,

---

165 The Leitz Camera conceived by O. Barnack, a Leitz technician, between 1913 and 1920, was created with the idea of adopting perforated film. Presented in 1924, the format remains the most widespread even today among professional and amateur photographers.

166 First film made: *White Christmas* by Michael Curtiz.

thus the actual shot sometime included things that ought to be cut in projection: this explains why studio equipment sometimes appears (tracks or microphones in particular) which was obviously not part of the composition envisioned by the director, especially on TV or in video editions.

With the aim of replicating the impression of *scope* without having to rent the original material from Fox,[167] patents for anamorphic compression lenses multiplied all over the world in the years immediately afterwards. While other, more or less compressed, wide-screen filming systems were devised, they necessarily had to be compatible with 35mm film in the projection booth, even the stereophonic magnetic sound track was then attached to copies which also carried, in any case, a normal monophonic optical sound track. Finally, prefiguring what would happen with Dolby systems, MGM introduced a simulation of stereophonic sound, thanks to the decoding of sub audible frequencies directed by an integrator that distributed specific sound effects to different sources: *Perspecta Sound.* Within the context of this inexhaustible research, Italy could only produce a thrift-driven invention. In 1963, for Italian Technicolor, Giovanni Ventimiglia developed *Techniscope*,[168] a system where filming involved only half of the conventional frame; it was called 2P (i.e. engaging only two perforations). The rectangular frames (1:2.35) thus obtained were printed and then enlarged through an anamorphic lens into a normal positive scope image. This meant a 50% saving in negative film stock.[169]

Then in 1963, on the home stretch, Cinerama returned to the large format, developing an uncompressed positive and negative 70mm wide.[170] Apart from projections in the usual "few select theatres", it could still be reduced to normal 35mm positive copies.

167 Although the patent had already expired in 1927, Fox promoted the manufacture of the necessary lenses which were leased as needed together with the brand which covered all the technologies involved.

168 First film made: *Ieri, oggi, domani* by Vittorio De Sica.

169 The negative, instead, engaged three perforations and produced an aspect ratio of 1:2 that required a specific projector, or else it could be transferred anamorphically onto normal copies, again managing to cut costs, this was the core idea behind Univisium patented by Vittorio and Fabrizio Storaro in the mid-90s. The first film made using this format was *Flamenco* by Carlos Saura (1995).

170 First film made: *It's a Mad, Mad, Mad, Mad World* by Stanley Kramer.

There were many systems based on this technology, from *Todd-Ao*[171] (1954), to *Technirama 70*[172] (1959) and other compatible systems, but they have since become obsolete. Nevertheless, there have been still quite a number of films made, even recently, that were shot in 35mm and then inflated in 70mm for quality vision in those cinemas which still have the necessary equipment.[173] Finally, since 1970, the latest system to provide the ultimate quality experience in dedicated cinemas is IMAX; it runs a 70mm film horizontally as in *VistaVision*, with fifteen perforations per frames and multichannel stereophonic sound.

But sound has been the sector in which cinema has been able to further refine its expressive potential. Beginning from the reduction of so-called *background noise* during playback: in 1965 Ray Dolby developed his *Dolby A* system which started in the music industry and was soon taken on in film too. In 1974, he made a stereophonic system adapted to the width of the optical column that matched the overall quality of the magnetic system. Two films, in particular, convinced cinemas to install the *Dolby Stereo* decoder (while, if need, the optical column could still be read in mono): *Star Wars* and *Apocalypse Now*. Then, from 1990, a definitive turning point came, and not just for Dolby: digital. This umpteenth recycling of 35mm required space to print, in addition to the usual stereo-mono compatible optical column, thousands and thousands of "compressed" pixels to be interpreted by a sort of computer that selected the channels to be amplified. Dolby fit the pixels into the space between the perforations (Dolby Stereo SR.D), while Sony chose the outer edge of the film (SDDS). Finally, next to the optical track Universal transcribed a very thin time-code[174] that drove an external CD player: in *Jurassic Park* (1993). It

---

171 First film made: *Oklahoma!* by Fred Zinnemann.

172 First film made: *Sleeping Beauty,* by Walt Disney.

173 From *Apocalypse Now* (1979) by Francis Ford Coppola to *Dick Tracy* (1990) by Warren Beatty: Vittorio Storaro, "author" of photography, attended personally to the printing for all the films in which he was involved, the copies to be distributed around the world were entrusted to Technicolor in Rome.

174 A progressive time code in professional television supports which precisely identifies every point of the recording (down to the single *frame*). As of 1990 it was also available in film, both as a code inserted during shooting and in a progressive numbering after development. Such encodings are useful for multiple operations, from digital editing, to the identification of the original portions of negative and print grading or timing.

seemed that cinema was seeking yet another sound dimension (DTS), and it recalled, moreover, the first system that officially permitted cinema to speak. Obviously, it was no longer a question of synchronising a turntable with a projector as was the case of the *Vitaphone*. Now information technology was guiding the whole process, if the CD player suffered the slightest failure, it would instantaneous return to reading and reproducing the old, still acceptable and reliable, optical column.

When considering this expansion in the dimension of sound, we cannot forget the attempts made over the years to enrich viewing with a third dimension. The idea of replicating human vision actually anticipates the advent of photography. In 1832, the English physicist Charles Weastone described *stereoscopy*; as of 1851, it was applied by David Brewster using decodable drawings and a special viewer. *Stereoscopy* enjoyed extraordinary success in the 1800s, its diffusion overlapping with that of newly born photograph. Towards the end of that century it was even spectacularised through Magic Lantern projections employing *anaglyph*, a system that allowed the simultaneous superimposed projection of two images taken at the interpupillary distance and coloured with two complementary colours, red and green or red and blue: a spectator wearing glasses with lenses of the same colours thus experienced a three-dimensional effect. Occasional experiments aside, it was in the 20s that cinema started to apply methodologies and systems, though without achieving great results. However, they tried again and again for years. Especially when it became possible to make the images selective through the introduction of *polarisation* (using special lenses with an imperceptible but dense set of parallel, horizontally and vertically aligned lines) lowering brightness only slightly and therefore allowing the use of colour. In the 1950s, the film industry also used *stereoscopy* in an attempt to combat the rise of television: both the version already previously experimented with *anaglyphs,* two overlapping monochromatic images (*Creature from the Black Lagoon*), and the most recent complex and colourful type, based on polarised light (*Bwana Devil* by Arch Oboler, 1953). The technology, initially synchronising two cameras and two projectors, was particularly complex to handle in cinemas, but it became simpler over time and eventually used prisms to code and project the two images with slightly different angles on a single frame. In 1983, *Jaws 3*, the penultimate hunt for the ferocious predator renewed its proceeds thanks to a revival of *stereoscopy*. However, to be truly enchanted by actual three-dimensional effects, one had to wait for the brief but highly suggestive documentaries given in the few existing IMAX 3D theatres (experiments started in 1978).

The deterioration of film

The magical paradox underlying the very existence of cinema is that *celluloid film*, it's very essence, is among the most fragile and delicate of industrial products: with remarkable ease it can disintegrate, be scratched or broken, and moreover, it can deteriorate in quality and not only in its purely photographic nature. Historically, celluloid means cellulose nitrate, a *colourless, transparent plastic* on the one hand and on the other a *highly flammable* material that can even self-combust. Celluloid is, moreover, chemically unstable: from the moment of its manufacture a very slow but inescapable molecular modification begins, producing sulphur dioxide and other gases: a progressive degradation that seems vowed to self-annihilation. The emulsion is spread on this strip of organic plastic *support*, in other words, the sensitive material composed of silver salts that is suspended in a gelatin which adheres to the celluloid. Initially, its sensitivity to light was very low and the gelatin-silver salt mixture could not encode the entire visual spectrum in black and white. It was only at the beginning of the 20s that *panchromatic* emulsion was universally adopted so that all the colours of the spectrum could be reproduced in shades of grey.

Given the initial inaccuracy of laboratory equipment, during development and printing the *fixing* bath (the most delicate operation because it definitively blocks the image) was not always performed correctly, it could consequently lead to a rapid deterioration in the emulsion which, over time, could become even worse because the gases produced by the unstable celluloid support.

There is a further complication connected to a lesser-known aspect of the entire silent era. Except in sporadic cases, those films were not distributed in black and white, but conforming to popular taste (in painting and printing), they were coloured, though not in a very natural manner. The copies, of course, were coloured, except for specific and very problematic experiments that rarely reached the public, colour systems in *filming* and *printing* still belonged to the future. Thus the colouring of shots or sequences was done with small brushes, detail by detail, on parts of each single frame (in 1906 the procedure was simplified and industrialised using matrices to apply various colours by machine = *stencil*); or a uniform colour was applied by immersion (*imbibition*) or by dyeing the silver (*toning* and/or *mordent toning*). In imbibition the *scene* was uniformly coloured as it was applied to the support itself, while dye toning changed the colour only in those parts revealed by the silver leaving the support itself transparent. Naturally, it was possible to combine these techniques to obtain complex colours. However, since *toning* and *mordent toning* were the result of a series of chemical reactions, they could trigger other phenomena led to some permanent damage to the emulsion over time.

Finally, the *support*, although reliable and rather resistant to mechanical traction, was still being used in semi-professional equipment and could be hindered by small imperfections that could scratch and weaken the celluloid until it broke.

In short, this very essence of cinema, conserved and perpetuated the seeds of its own destruction.

Many of these defects have been eliminated over the years, first and foremost thanks to increasingly improved and reliable machinery. Secondly, a pure non-flammable *acetate* support was soon developed which, though more fragile and more expensive, was used almost exclusively for educational films to be screened in venues lacking in adequate fire prevention measures. Then, from the 50s onward, a new *cellulose triacetate* (finally chemically stable as well) was gradually adopted all over the world. Today, we have come further with non-organic esters (*polyester*, *elstar* and others), which are practically indeformable and indestructible supports (the basic materials also used for audio and video recording).

While the stability of emulsions had been ensured for black and white images, (when treated and conserved in an exemplary manner under controlled temperature and relative humidity), as of the mid-30s problems arose when the various colour systems gradually began to be developed. Indeed, among the now outdated classic Technicolor formats from the 40s to the 60s, not a single one exists that can ensure stability and durability, neither in negatives nor copies (indeed the situation is similar for cinema's mother/sister photography). Pending the completion of IT transfers which would seems to guarantee eternity in digital coding in the near future, the only possibility means of stabilising the chromatic data consists in decoding the three basic colours and entrusting them to silver emulsions (i.e. black and white: in jargon they are called *silver copies*). This operation itself is very expensive, and the costs are further increased by a much more complex storage process since the quantity of materials is thus increased.

As we know, the *cans* are the metal containers (once made of cardboard and today plastic) for transporting and storing film. Their capacity varies, although we have seen that at the beginning of the 20th century the industry made a standard 1000 feet (approximately 305m) the symbolic value of a base unit: the *reel*. There is, of course, an amazing difference between the original negative, the painstaking editing that composes the work print (with the various soundtracks – words, music, noises – still separated), which is no longer necessary today thanks to computer editing, and the positive for screening. Of all these meters (or feet) of film, the most important is, of course, the original negative (an *assembly* of dozens and dozens of pieces of film), which needs to be handled and safeguarded with every possible precaution. We should remember that the negative in the silent era was tailored to eventual further colouring and various graphic codes identified the positioning of writings and captions within shots; the copies for circulation had to be glued together shot by shot and the result was very fragile. By the time sound came, progress in assembly systems has reduced the risk to this perishable original caused by mechanical damage such as scratching or, worse, breakage. Sound was initially recorded on alternative supports such as discs (*Vitaphone*), and then entrusted to other films of the same dimension, using different technologies (like the *Movietone* optical sound track and the post-war magnetic sound track), and finally, on professional audio-cassettes of which the DAT (*Digital Audio*

Tape) became the consolidated format in the 90s (since it can be synchronised with film, video and the various digital standards).

Given its instability, the first support *cellulose nitrate* is the most degradable. Opening the aforementioned *cans*, which may have rusted because of prolonged inadequate conservation, you may find reels that are wet and sticky (like *jam*), even compacted into a single mass; or else hard and calcified coils that are impossible to play. Despite the fact that appropriate procedures exist, it is not always possible to restore deteriorated films to a point that they can be viewed again. Even in the case of the more stable *triacetate* support, the so-called *vinegar syndrome* can lead to such deterioration.

Special effects: from black and white to colour

Thanks to better quality materials, the *tricks* employed in cinema, the principles of which were established by Méliès, were being constantly improved and refined. *Matting* and *overlapping* continued to be systematically used, though when colour became possible they became more problematic as the emulsions had such low sensitivity that the use of *transparency*, for example, became difficult. And while *painting on glass* and even *fixed mattes* continued to be the basis of set design, the biggest problem was to find a system, similar to the *Dunning process* in black and white, for *movable mattes* and *counter mattes* so that figures could be inserted, including those made of cardboard. At the end of the 30s, Technicolor developed the *blue screen* or *blue back*. Blue was identified as the easiest colour to separate from other primaries and the most manageable in obtaining *matte-silhouettes* thanks to high-contrast prints that could make the image in the foreground transparent. This renewed effect debuted in *The Thief of Baghdad* (1940) – a film, moreover, in which the whole repertoire of effects was exploited to the maximum, and in colour, from *miniatures* to *full-scale reconstructions* including giant hairpieces.[175] Over the years other systems appeared with actors feigning actions in front of a neutral

---

175 A foot and a hand of the enormous genie of the lamp, in many ways similar to those of the cinema's most famous prewar beast, *King Kong* by Merian C. Cooper and Ernst B. Schoedsack in 1933 with special effects by Willis O'Brien and not only...

screen, illuminated, for example, by infrared light or sodium vapour. The latter process was the ingenuous creation of Ub Iwerks, an animator and former partner of Walt Disney, who, after an unsuccessful autonomous venture, returned to Disney to devote himself to technology. In 1943, Ub made Donald Duck dance with Aurora Miranda and other Latin American beauties in the colour film *The Three Caballeros*,[176] thanks to his particular *optical printer* that facilitated the superimposition of two separate sources. In 1964, on the other hand, it was *Mary Poppins* that demonstrated the progress attained in the management of several cartoons, thanks to the *Sodium Vapor Process* (or *Sodium Travelling Matte Process*). This system, together with other technologies continuously fine-tuned by Iwerks over more than thirty years, was to become as indispensable as it was invisible in creating immanent terror in Alfred Hitchcock's *The Birds*. To avoid parasitic reflections that sometimes smudged the outline of characters with a bluish aura (an imperfection in the management of *mattes*), over time they learnt to use a wider film surface (70mm, VistaVision, etc.) which was then reduced when printing the final negatives. But other paths were also explored, first of all an ingenious use of *scotchlite*, a material developed by 3M (also used to make road signs), which instead of absorbing light, reflects it almost entirely.

Between 1950 and 1957, the patent for *front-projection* bounced between America and Europe. It was perfected in Europe (thanks to Henri Alekan and Georges Gérard, two great French cinematographers) with the adoption of a reflex screen made of millions of tiny silicon beads instead of scotchlite's original mosaic of embossed micro-prisms on a plastic base. The previously prepared background images are projected on a semi-reflecting mirror set at 45° to the reflex screen. Illuminated slightly more intensely than the projected image and in such a way as not to produce shadows, the actors perform in front of the screen. The camera, placed perfectly in line in front of the screen, frames the actors through the mirror and against the background (whether fixed or moving) reflected by the *scotchlite*. The first time *front-projection*

---

176 The film, under art supervisors Mary Blair, Kenneth Anderson and Robert Cormack, was made between 1943 and 1944 and was released in Italy in 1949.

was used, in 1967, it became relatively easy to have Jane Fonda (Barbarella) flying[177] in the arms of John Philip Law (the angel Pygar); and likewise, the following year, to create the primitive setting for the initial clash of the apes and the miniature of the space station in *2001: A Space Odyssey*. And, speaking of *2001*, we should remember that cinema's *special effects* are not only *photographic* and/or *optical tricks*, but every element capable of creating exemplary images whether real or unreal. The interior of the circular space station in *2001*, where gravity appeared to be suspended (characters walking from upright to upside down ...), was set into a sturdy outer shell that could be rotated and the camera along with it. Thus, since the camera moves but the projector is stationary (an essential law in cinema, though less self-evident than it may seem), on the screen the viewers see a fixed frame. In reality however, they have turned 360° along with the entire set, while the actor (like the Fred Astaire who dances across walls and ceilings in *Royal Wedding* by Stanley Donen) has been faithful to the law of gravity even though it does not seem so. In addition to these scenographic and technological devices, *special effects* also include all the instruments designed to produce rain (tanks and high-pressure pumps), lightning (carbon arc lamps handled by an electrician), snow (tufts of cotton, industrial salt mixed with polystyrene or grains of mothballs on the ground, or foam fired from a kind of cannon), fog (black and white smoke cookies, burning charcoal and incense, but also heated and va-porised mineral oil): again, whatever atmospheric effect is needed, the principle is to produce and control it, instead of seeking the real thing. Similarly, fire is always produced and controlled using gas in cylinders; and water, when real, is channelled from huge reservoirs through shaped and directed waterways, or else created virtually with mirrors and, in the case of epochal floods,[178] by the optical printer. Accidents, whether cars, ships or airplanes, are recreated in phases using reduced-scale models while details are often progressively deformable, realistic and in real scale thanks to the acrobatics of *stuntmen*. For blood and gore, there are other

177 *Barbarella*, 1967, by Roger Vadim, based on the comic strip by Jean-Claude Forest.
178 The parting of the Red Sea in *The Ten Commandments*, by Cecil B. DeMille, 1957).

special effects, a cross between *make-up*[179] (wigs, hairpieces, pros-
thetics ...) and mechanical effects using puppets (either imaginary
or casts taken from the actors, made of *latex*, and operated with
external wires or moved internally) activated live *outside the frame*
and using a variety of automated systems (*Animatronics*). But
when the blood comes from a bullet or an explosion, the maxi
or mini charge is entrusted to *pyrotechnic effects*, sometimes even
attached to the actor's body, ripping apart plastic containers that
produced the effect; the *slow motion* squirting effect became a
stylistic cipher in the work of directors such as Arthur Penn[180] or
Sam Peckinpah.[181] Furthermore, there are materials that can be
consumed or broken without danger, such as tea for whiskey or
modelled crystallised sugar (bottles, glasses), sheets of glass nowadays are made with synthetic hardener for paint. And, going by
the credits at the end of *Titanic*, it seems to be never-ending.

Editing and dubbing

The sound era finally rationalised editing which had previously
been not much more than a process of checking transparency
manually.[182] Later, takes became more easily identifiable thanks
to writing on a small blackboard included at the beginning of
each shot. The clapperboard was born. At the beginning it was
silent, the hinged clapstick was added later, its sharp dry snap was
a useful signal for the synchronisation of sound and image. The
support with images and the one with sounds (first optical and
then magnetic) were strictly separated during the stages of editing
and mixing. To tell the truth, since the end of the 19th century,
individual viewing devices used for controlling shots did exist
(such as the Aléthorama[183] which employed rotating mirrors), but
they were not widely available. The instrument that is synonymous
with editing, the Moviola, was designed by the German immigrant

---

179 Makeup in the sense of cosmetics, but the hair stylist is yet another specialist in this specific
   department.

180 *Bonnie and Clyde*, 1967.

181 *The Wild Bunch*, 1969.

182 See Riccardo Redi, *Montaggio senza moviola,* in "Immagine, note di storia del cinema", n. 1,
   1981, p. 2.

183 See Gian Carlo Bertolina: *Un antenato della moviola l'alerorama*, in "Immagine, note di
   storia del cinema", new series n. 24, summer–autumn 1993, p. 22.

Iwan Serrurier and was patented in the USA in April 1919. This upright machine could carry out precise work on the positive image before it was synchronised with the sound track. Although the Moviola is still in use today, with subsequent improvements, it met with valid competition in Europe in the so-called *flatbed editor*, a natural evolution from the basic *light box* used for controlling copies: a table with two large plates for viewing the film horizontally. Italy was among the developers of the most brilliant subsequent developments:[184] an optical compensation system inserted for viewing while the film was running, and various sound heads (optical at first and then also magnetic). An electric motor was added that runs at the standard 24 f/s and at variable speeds both forward and reverse. Up to 4 different sources (images and/or sounds) which are mechanically interchangeable (using sprockets) can be handled at the same time. Thus, for each positive it becomes possible to independently synchronise the three soundtracks (dialogue, music, noises) which are need for the final mix of the answer print (for re-recording) and the composite assembly (incorporating sound and image) of the final positive copy. The *dialogue* track remains separate for dubbing on foreign-language markets while the mix of music and noises, the so-called international sound track, cannot be altered. From the outset of the sound era, *dialogue* has implied dubbing, at least in Italy. That is: dubbing began as soon as technology was able to function separately on a variety of sound sources. At the beginning, when there was music underlining the dialogue, they had to be performed simultaneously. Versions of the same film in different languages for the international markets were entrusted to different actors and even different directors. And even if it was possible to print a summary translation of the dialogues relatively early on, Italy soon becomes the Mecca of dubbing (a decision initially taken by Benito Mussolini), and remains so today. This practice, which

---

184 There was another, equally brilliant, Italian invention which soon spread throughout the world. Until the 1960s, to glue pieces of film together a slender part of the gelatin had to be removed so it could be attached to the next piece using an acetone-based adhesive. The Italian editor Leo Catozzo was allergic to that particular chemical and in the late 50s he designed and produced a *press* that used adhesive tape which, with due precautions, could also be removed. Adopted universally (and even copied despite the patent), the Catozzo press allows editors to avoid direct intervention on the frames, so that they are not lost when there are second thoughts about a cut.

might otherwise be at best tolerated when not openly deplored, has enjoyed the creative approval of geniuses such as Federico Fellini. Thanks to the introduction of the time code that facilitates the identification of selected shots, all these assembly processes, dubbing, mixing and editing, have been done for years now through computer programs such as AVID.

Developing and printing

This fundamental sector of the industry became more complicated at first by sound initially and then colour, but ultimately they actually led to its rationalisation. New departments were set up dedicated to *special effects* using optical printers, however, these have long since become computerised stations equipped with extremely powerful processors. They then focused mainly on the automation and acceleration of operations.

Projection

Through necessity the *Vitaphone* led to equipment that connected a projector to a special turntable; but it was a short-lived solution. Projectors had a standard constant speed (24 f/s was sufficient to have a two-bladed shutter instead of the original three) and were equipped with a *sound head* connected to an amplifier and a large speaker behind the screen. As had happened in the film studio, the sound era also called for special attention to acoustics in cinemas. Over the following years equipment in cinemas had to adapt to new discoveries that had, nevertheless, to be accommodated on the same standard 35mm surface (except for unusual colour experiments or alternative formats). Firstly, the various scopes needed modified aperture gates and longer focal lenses than *normal* as well as lenses that decompressed the image back to its regular rectangular format. Then, *widescreen* required other aperture gates and other focal lenses, this led to the addition of a rotating turret which, once focus had been stabilised, was set in position according to the required aspect ratio. Over time, even these functions became automatic. With the introduction of 70mm, some projectors were equipped with a sort of "by-pass": an interchangeable pressure-plate lens and Maltese cross block (the heart of the machine's intermittent movement), apart form that the other drive elements were designed to accommodate both the normal and double formats. Except for the gradual introduction of new sound heads in a variety of positions as technology became more refined, the only real novelty, which dates back to the mid-50s, was the introduction of the Xenon lamp in place of the carbon arc lamp. Despite the fact that the first large-screen television projection systems had already been developed in the 1930s, the *eidophor* was only used occasionally. It was employed for the first time in Europe during the 1952 Venice Film Festival, to broadcast live from the Lido to Cinema Rossini in the historic centre of Venice, and it was used frequently between 1955 and 1956 (was it perhaps because audiences would have deserted the evening screenings had they not been able to watch the evening's episode of *Lascia o raddoppia?* ...). In the 60s, the first *cam programmers* driven by punched tape were introduced, making all the operations in the projection booth automatic. While the main feature rewound (ten minutes at most) the screen was occupied by newsreels and trailers. In multiplexes today the same copy can be used for different and adjoining screens.

Chapter Fourteen

Cinema and digital

The computer has arrived!

The computer was introduced into the film industry to programme and hence repeat complex mechanical movements with absolute precision. The *Dykstraflex* (named after its inventor John Dykstra, but subsequently also *Computer Motion Control* or *Computer Controlled Camera*), based on the principle of relative motion, created the chases and battles in *Star Wars*. The camera moved in towards and away from models of spaceships fixed on supports against strictly blue backgrounds, replicating motion with identical, synchronised speed, perspective, etc. thus obtaining basic images that could be composited (whether in deep space or everyday life). At that time there was also talk of computers in the world of Japanese animation; in reality, however, at most the computer managed a database to identify a succession of guidelines in drawings so as to replicate specific actions and adapt them to the robot in question. Research continued into improving *effects* that were already known: the ZOPTIC *(Zoom Optic)*, for example, perfected in England by Zoran Persic, equipped both camera and projector in *front projection* processes with an inversely synchronised zoom, creating highly evocative images of Superman (Christopher Reeve) in flight.[185]

The computer's real entry into the treatment of images, however, came about thanks to experiments exploiting the technological exchange between cinema and TV. In 1973, to save on costs, an

---

185 *Superman,* by Richard Donner, 1978.

attempt was made to make a celluloid copy[186] of the poorly-defined NTSC television signal (525 lines)[187] of a scandalous theatrical revue entitled *Oh! Calcutta* featuring actors in their "birthday suits". For much the same reason Jacques Tati filmed his last film *Parade* on *magnetic tape* the same year. In 1980, Michelangelo Antonioni became fascinated with the idea of using television technology to control and manipulate colours while filming and he designed and produced the *The Mystery of Oberwald*[188] on video, though the final destination was the cinema screen. In this rather evocative case, the limit lies precisely in the grainy definition of the television image which becomes even worse when enlarged on the cinema screen. And while Francis Ford Coppola and Vittorio Storaro exploited everything technology had to offer, from the PC to video-recording, to organise, rehearse and perform each section of *One From the Heart* (1982), an experiment necessarily shot in studio, it was up to the Japanese television giant Sony to embark on the definitive contamination. Sony and NHK (*Nippon Hoso Kiokai*, the Japanese Broadcasting agency), believed it would be sufficient to double the lines (1125), adopt a widescreen (16/9 instead of 4/3) and introduce stereo sound, to be able to use video recording in all the phases of shooting and post-production, and then transfer the finished product to celluloid – until enormous ultra-flat liquid crystal displays (LCD: *Liquid Cristal Display*)[189] could be developed for cinemas.

With the introduction of *High Definition* or HDTV in 1980, the idea of abandoning celluloid began to take root in the film industry. Vittorio Storaro was the first cinematographer to experiment with

---

186 Since the advent of TV, the only means of recording TV images had been to transfer them onto film using a device called a *kinescope*. It was only in 1956 that the first VTR (*Video Tape Recorder*) was perfected in the USA by Ginsberg and Dolby of the Ampex Corporation, using 2-inch magnetic tape with mobile heads. By 1973, video recording had become a reality even for colour TV.

187 The NTCS *National Television System Committee* (nicknamed *Never the same colour* because of its initial unreliability) was adopted in the USA and Japan, broadcasting at a standard 525 lines; instead the German PAL (*Phase Alternation Line*) system, with 625 lines was used mostly in Europe. The French SECAM (*Séquentiel Couleur à Mémoire*) is conceptually different.

188 Based on *L'Aigle à deux têtes* by Jean Cocteau.

189 Liquid crystals that change orientation in response to electromagnetic fields. They are arranged in RGB (red, green, blue) cells that define a pixel and are the basis of backlit screens of varying definition and quality.

this delicate equipment which he brought to Venice to test in a less than ideal climate; Giuliano Montaldo's *Arlecchino*, filmed during a gloomy winter in 1982, was successful to a certain degree. And it was likewise with subsequent experiments, always co-managed by RAI, which included a feature film in 1986: *Giulia e Giulia* by Peter Del Monte, in Trieste, another humid setting. Few other directors (Wenders and Greenaway) experimented with the uninspiring quality achieved transferring video to film, even the direct reproduction of the master video itself seemed problematic: on the correct screen HDTV is refined and high quality, it remains a television standard and is distributable only by satellite. As research progressed *plasma*[190] replaced LCDs, though definition increased the technology has never managed to produce an ultra-flat screen of sufficient quality for cinema venues. Attention shifted, therefore, to other devices, initiating a race to perfect the video projector. Meanwhile, following the logic behind HDTV equipment led to a system for scanning film images at one frame per second and a resolution close to 3500 lines (Kodak's *High Resolution Electronic Intermediate System*): in 1989, Sony and Ampex introduced digital on the professional video recording market. Thus, after the early attempts with limited use (*Tron*, by Steven M. Lisberger, from 1982) the computer had become fully enabled in the processing of cinematographic images by catering for the technological logic of TV. This is also due to the fact that, in the meantime, good old *Kodak* had continued to perfect a means of bringing temporarily digitalised, computer processed data back to film: the initial laser beam (later infrared) system created three black and white matrices, one for each fundamental colour, thus reconstructing a colour negative of "para-photographic" quality. Experimentation, which started again in 1988 with Ron Howard's *Willow*, moved into every field of *special effects*, working on longer and longer shots as computer memories expanded. And while *Who Framed Roger Rabbit?* (still in 1988) became the triumph of the optical printer, used by the technicians at *Industrial Light and Magic* (founded by George Lucas) to create light and shadow with

190 Plasma technology is related to liquid crystals, it replicates a network of cells enclosed in a mixture of noble gases which reproduce the entire colour range when stimulated by electrical impulses.

at least 15 steps per frame, lending three-dimensional life to Jessica and the other cartoon heroes designed by Richard Williams, from this moment on, however, it was to be the *chroma key* (a television systems which selectively cancels red, green and blue[191]) that can almost automatically reinvent *mattes* and *counter mattes* for *composite images* of unmatched quality that has gradually replaced *historical optical effects* and much more. Automatically, because information technology allows you to manage, perfect and customise 2D and 3D graphics programmes, even going so far as to recycle (though only for a few moments) an actor's body, as with Brandon Lee in *The Crow* (1994). 2D graphics have enhanced the expressive qualities of cartoons while 3D has almost completely replaced stop motion animation with puppets and objects.

Film: recovery and restoration

In recent years, even the non-specialist has had the opportunity to learn more about that branch of cinema defined as *silent film*[192] (though only for historiographical convenience and classificatory utility) thanks to specialised festivals, monographic exhibitions, events devoted to silent film or individual public screenings of period films, appropriately restored and presented with their musical accompaniment.

In the 1930s there were four European film archives (in Sweden, France, the United Kingdom and Germany), today almost every European country has at least one. In some countries, such as Italy, the United Kingdom, Spain and France there are also a number of important regional archives specifically focused on the history of a community or a specific area. Regardless of whether they preserve and restore surviving films (nitrates), many of them are also information points, libraries and presentation facilities (housing cinemas and sometimes even permanent exhibitions).[193]

Each copy of a film recounts its own history dating back to the era in which it was produced. A film from the first decade of the 20th century was filmed and elaborated in a radically different way from a work produced in the 20s.

191 While red is too close to skin colour to be reliable, green and blue instead can both be exploited successfully. The *key* works with two shots at the same time, one direct and the other pre-recorded or, more simply, in post-production, with different *contributions* that have been filmed or elaborated or in a variety of ways.

192 Gianni Rondolino in the preface to Paolo Cherchi Usai, *Una passione infiammabile*, UTET Libreria, Torino 1991, p. VII.

193 Ghislaine Jenson, "Le cineteche in Europa", in Luisa Comencini and Matteo Pavesi (ed.) *Restauro, conservazione e distruzione del film*, Quaderni Fondazione Cineteca Italiana, Editrice Il Castoro, Milan 2001, p. 34

> The technologies used while shooting, processing in laboratories and the film stocks themselves have constantly changed over a hundred years. The history of film technology therefore leaves its mark on every film. But the vicissitudes of each copy also modify it as a physical entity.[194]

The idea of a *museum* or *film archive*[195] dates back to 1898, but at that time was seen as a *privileged historical source*, similar to a library but certainly not dedicated to fiction but to the documentation of reality. In the USA, from the origins of cinema to the 1920s (in the absence of specific legislation and akin to other deposits already being made), the need for copyright led to the creation of an extraordinary collection of printed copies on photographic paper at the *Library of Congress* in Washington. These copies (the *Paper Print Collection*) were rediscovered in the 1950s and hundreds of works were rephotographed frame by frame (of the thousands that were deposited, however, many were damaged beyond repair), many were works that would have otherwise been lost (including films by Griffith and Méliès). But this was an anomaly in the overall panorama as only some specific topics were deemed worthy material for a film collection (science, particularly medicine, war, etc.). It was only at the turn of the 30s – probably also thanks to the presumed uselessness of silent films, seen as obsolete with the advent of sound – that the idea of safeguarding film material for historical and cultural reasons began to spread publicly and privately. In 1933, a film critic established the *Svenska Filmsanfundet* in Stockholm and in the 1940s it became a state institution; in 1934 the *Reichsfilmarchiv* was founded by the German government as was the nucleus of educational works at the VGIK, the Moscow Film School; in 1935 two private entities were set up: the *film department* at the *Museum of Modern Arts* (*MOMA*) in New York, meanwhile in Milan, Mario Ferrari, Luigi Comencini, Alberto Lattuada, but also Luciano Emmer, Giulio Macchi, Luigi Veronesi and others, sifting through piles celluloid

---

194 Gian Luca Farinelli and Nicola Mazzanti, (ed.), *Il cinema ritrovato, teoria e metodologia del restauro cinematografico*, Grafis Edizioni, Bologna 1994, p. 47.

195 It was Bolesław Matuszewski, a Polish immigrant in France, who first launched the idea. See Giovanni Grazzini, *La memoria negli occhi, Bolesław Matuszewski: un pioniere del cinema*, Carocci, Rome 1999.

in deposits and basements that were destined for the landfill, set aside those masterpieces that today are part of the immense heritage of the *Italian Film Archive*. But, we should also point out that the *Venice Biennale* had already recognised the artistic nature of cinema by founding the Venice Film Festival in 1932. Again in 1935, the first convention of these nascent film archives took place in Berlin, laying the foundation for an association (*FIAF, the International Federation of Film Archives*) which was established in Paris in 1938. They began to deal with issues that continue to remain partly unsolved even today, such as copyright, and consequently accessibility to works that have been preserved, and the technologies used for their restoration. While continuing to be established all over the world, Film Archives have to contend with issues of funding on the one hand, and on the other with a certain exclusivist sense of possession that is incomprehensible, yet quite typical of some private collectors. What was lost almost immediately, especially for technical reasons, was the practice of colour. In particular, when a more stable, non-flammable support was finally universally adopted, the race began (as yet incomplete[196]) to save works on nitrate making them available only in unsatisfactory black and white copies. Indeed, it is one thing to *duplicate* and therefore, generically *save*, it is quite another to *restore*, which today means to recover a work's originality, the conditions of its first public release. The rediscovery and the consequent re-introduction of colour has been crucial to this,[197] today it is widely applied with a variety of technologies that have developed into actual schools of thought from the philological point of view.

While the worst irreversible mistakes for silent films might be to fail to respect the original format (for example reprinting using a matte that is smaller although replicating the basic aspect ratio, and off-centre to accommodate the soundtrack), when it comes

---

196 The slogan repeated over the years has been *Nitrate can't wait*. It has been interpreted even excessively in the past by some archives that made poor quality copies of original nitrates on safe supports and then destroyed the "dangerous" inflammable originals.

197 The widespread use of colour on TV has increased the demand for colour film causing laboratories to reconvert their equipment and this in turn has reduced costs. Thus, Film Archives, which are normally very poor, have been able to request work that respects the restoration of coloured originals.

to *imbibition* and *toning*, alternative systems have been developed[198] to the actual replication of the original technologies, however successful. While knowing that all the colour material is at risk, as it deteriorates with time, some prefer to obtain a colour negative and then print copies on a relative positive (a mandatory operation when dealing with manual or *stencil* colours). Instead, Noël Desmet, of the Cinémathèque Royale du Belgique, has developed a method that starts out from a black and white duplicate and builds a negative that should stand the test of time. Based on the colours originally used, Desmet transfers the images onto colour film and retrieves the colours thanks to the filters in the printer. The required shade of colour for *toning* is chosen directly from the various lights in the coloured printer; two steps are needed for *imbibition*, the first for the basic black and white image and afterwards *flashing*[199] to replicate the original monochrome.

Today, every restoration project ought to start from a survey of all the surviving copies and, hopefully, though this is not always possible, an examination of all the available documents (*screenplays*, *censorship visas* and details of *captions*, etc.) including the *score* of the original music, if it exists. These are very complex operations which have gained fresh impetus thanks to the *Lumière Project*, a celebration of the Centenary of Cinema, that involved all the European archives. They are screened in those few select cinemas that can ensure the correct aspect ratio and speed (usually limited to specialised events such as *Le Giornate del Cinema Muto*[200] in Pordenone, the first such event in Italy and a forerunner in the world – followed by *Cinema Ritrovato* in Bologna – or else in *film archives*). As we have already seen, until the sound era, no standard had been adopted and each film had its own specific

198 At the *Narodni Filmovy Archiv* in Prague, directed by Valdimir Opela, there is a device for the imbibition of up to six colours that directly transfers the dye to the copy without having to cut it into pieces.

199 Exposure to a very low light source to increase the sensitivity of an emulsion, reducing its contrasts. The negative is normally printed on a *flashed* emulsion in a second phase, to minimise blacks and obtain very saturated and bright colours.

200 This festival's foundation in 1982 basically coincided with a new generation within the film archives, a sign of their willingness to open their doors to the outside world and seek collaboration in restoration projects. At the same time, scholars became more aware of a pressing need to access materials, to view works that had often previously been thought missing or inaccessible except for the sometimes imperfect recall of those who had.

speed, though slower than today (14 f/s upwards, while sound films run at 24f/s) – speed can only be accurately determined from the rhythm the musical accompaniment, when it exists.

The same rigour and philology underpin the restoration of films from the sound era (the end of the 20s onwards) shortly before the definitive arrival of colour (late 30s). Despite the costs, the contribution of information technology is increasingly important in recovering the originality of both sound and colour. This is also because progress has brought new discoveries over the years that has rendered many other systems obsolete. Therefore, it is essential to keep up with technology so as to recover the original charm of each single work.

Many restorations, especially in the USA, have been carried out for the television and/or the *home-video* market. Leaving aside unfortunate falsifications (in particular *colouring* films which were originally black and white and the use of *PAN & SCAN* which cuts the aspect ratio of films made for wide screen formats like *Cinemascope* and other similar systems) very often these operations start out from original materials which, thanks to television systems and computer technology, have the opportunity to repair deteriorated sound, colour or image. This does not mean saving the original work, it means transferring it to another support, even when employing optimal criteria. The same applies for transfers to video tape, the obsolete digital laser disk and today's very popular DVD (*Digital Versatile Disc*). These are more than legitimate operations that help, among other things, the availability not only of good cinema but also of important documentary material preserved on film at various times. Compared to black and white film (which can manage the coding of the three fundamental colours), some doubt remains about the strength and durability of these new supports. Also because their quality has not yet stood the test of time, and, moreover, as their progress continues to evolve day by day, so does their use and experimentation.

From silver to pixel

Without those images on film of dramas, adventures, comedies and events of humanity and nature there would be no cinema; there would be no subject-matter for the history of cinema; there would be no film studies. In its place would be either still images (photography) or fleeting ones (electronics). The point is confirmed by video: a civilisation that is prey to the nightmare of its visual memory has no further need of cinema. For cinema is the art of destroying moving images.[201]

Paolo Cherchi Usai, clear as ever, introduces us to what the film industry is almost demanding: the abolition of the cinema on film in favour of digital media. First of all, on the set, during the production phase, using *high-definition cameras* which are able, moreover, to shoot at 24P (24 progressive frames) just like film.[202] These *cameras,* with all the related *platforms* and equipment for *post-production* (a term, as we have already said, that includes all the post-shooting processes, especially as they can now be carried out using various computer programmes) were aimed at a final transfer to film. They first started from the complex tape recording systems of the HDTV format with 1125 lines (which is still in use in television as we have seen, albeit a niche market). Today there are various formats, they have still not been standardised as they are in constant and rapid evolution, nevertheless, the Sony HDCam 2, 2K 10801 format seems to be the most prevalent, recording in compressed format on tapes similar to the Betacam.

However, the development of increasingly sophisticated technologies for video projection (in particular *DLP-Digital Light Processing* based on DMD matrices[203] with oscillating mirrors developed by Texas Instruments), is aiming with increasing determination to definitively replace celluloid in cinemas with optical or magnetic digital supports. Seeking maximum definition, in both filming and projection, the entire process is based on the decomposition of light with consequent coding and separate treatment of the three fundamental colours on three sensitive surfaces, thus tripling its potential.

201 P. Cherchi Usai, *L'ultimo spettatore, sulla distruzione del cinema*, Editrice Il Castoro, Milan 1999, p. 7.

202 It is perhaps worth noting that in countries where electricity is produced at 50 Hz the frame rate is 25 images (50 fields) per second, whereas at 60Hz (USA and others) the frame rate per second becomes 30 (60 fields). At 30 frames, HDTV provided a sort of compensation in the passage from video to film, an unfortunate expedient that does not yield accurate reproduction for abrupt or fast movements. Hence the need to restore the correct, universally adopted 24f/s in filming video destined for the cinema.

203 Digital Micromirror Device.

Supposing we could actually count the pixels in an image revealed by optical/chemical and non-optical/electronic systems: "the definition on a modern colour film can be estimated, in digital terms, at around 4K, in other words 12,750,000 pixels per frame".[204] Mario Calzini,[205] instead, points out that a standard PAL television image (the current Italian national system), broadcasting at 625 lines (only 576 are seen on the TV screen), has a resolution of 439,875 pixels, which rises to 2,348,974 or 1125 lines in high definition (HDTV). We know that by scanning, starting from 3,500 lines and progressing to even more precise systems, it has become possible to encode ever longer cinema shots (i.e. sets of frames each around 7 million pixels, approximately 2K), elaborate them with specific computer programs thanks to sets of computers (one computer alone cannot handle such a mass of data), and finally transfer them to simulated photographic quality on film. To abandon celluloid, then, what kind of signal does a video projector require? It is necessary to use a graphics card, not TV criteria (lines) to manage image quality on a computer. Graphic cards range from the now obsolete VGA (640 x 480 pixels) and SVGA (800 x 600) of the late 90s, to the XGA (1024 x 768) which is now the standard even in the most accessible video projection through the available matrices (LDC liquid crystal in simpler equipment, and DMD oscillating mirrors in more complex ones).

> ... some experimental screenings of the first episode of the new series of *Star Wars* have been organised using digital projectors showing a copy of the film transcribed on file (around 1000 GB) and stored on a hard-disc [...]. The second episode was released in about twenty cinemas equipped with digital projectors, including one in Italy. The digital projector's dimensions are equivalent to a traditional 35mm film. The technology is derived from trichromatic separation: each fundamental colour with matrix of 1280 x 1024 mirrors manages the different shades and intensities of that specific colour [...]. The resolution of a digital projector is currently around two thousand horizontal lines with contrast ratios of 1000:1.[206]

204 Giovanna Fossati, "Dai grani ai pixel: il digitale in cineteca", in L. Comencini and M. Pavesi (ed.) *Restauro, conservazione* ... cit., p. 114

205 Mario Calzini, *Cento anni di cinema al cinema*, ANEC, Associazione Nazionale Esercenti Cinema, Rome 1995.

206 Paolo Marocco, entry headed *Digitale, cinema* in Enciclopedia del cinema Treccani, vol. II, Rome, p. 324.

Compared to Paolo Marocco's precise synthesis (2003), very significant steps forward have been taken. And not only in the field of projection. Today, a device like the *Red One* has brought 4K – just a few months ago it seemed like technological hyperbole and exclusively for projection – within everyone's reach: a real camera designed for movement i.e. full and progressive frame by frame movement (not interlaced fields), recorded on a hard disk (not solid as yet, like small HD home movie cameras such as the Sony TG3, but video tape has seen its day). In 2007, the first 4K feature film was made using the DALSA Origin Camera: *Tempting Hyenas* by LeVar Burton. While in 2008 Steven Soderbergh, among others, used the *Red One* – which continues to increase it resolution despite being much less expensive and much more manageable (5K at the last European show) – for two works he brought to Cannes: *Che: Part One* and *Che: Part Two*. In short, the cycle has been completed. As we have already said, many of the subsequent processes (editing, audio, mixing, special effects ...) now generally come under the name post-production, since – ideally – just one device, the computer, accessing different programmes, can meet all the requirements. When bringing about such a radical revolution, it is important, not just for trivial historicism, not to lose sight of where we started from, in the hope of belying the hypothesis of "a civilisation that is prey to the nightmare of its visual memory" which, in the words of Cherchi Usai, "has no further need of cinema".

Progress or regression?

Probably the most brilliant intuition in the entire history of cinema was when Technicolor used the silver image as a printing matrix.[207] It enhanced the materiality inherent in the revelation of an image through the development process. Materiality: the development bath dissolves the unexposed parts of the light sensitive layer, creating greater and lesser reliefs and depressions that tend towards nothingness, since washing the still uncertain areas with fixer also stabilises vast portions of transparent support. Printing with similar chemical baths allows the projection copy, always composed of

207 Recalling Joseph-Nicéhore Niépce's idea of the Heliography a forerunner of photography.

reliefs and depressions, to be exposed to light. The silver scattered inside the stabilised emulsion is now reduced to a minimum, but it exists and has settled in such a random way as to vibrate constantly – but invisibly – even in the same areas as the frames flow by. Though not perceived, this constant dynamic fluctuation of real light from illuminating equipment is grasped subliminally. It lends depth to the projection, whether in the pure silver of black and white or layers of pigment reconstructing the likeness of colour on the screen. It is a convention to think of 4K resolution as being capable of returning 12,750,000 original pixels, instead the whole traditional optical-chemical process is almost tangible, certainly material. Digital, on the other hand, was conceived and is replicated as *texture*, a collection of increasingly small dots, increasingly numerous therefore, but regularly placed: CCDs for shooting, LCDs and DMDs for projection. These dots (always triple to accommodate red, green and blue) are apparently invisible but, even though light has come back to govern projections, they remain simulations of images, since to compensate for the impossibility of managing such an enormous mass of variable data in fractions of a second, compression, a factor that certainly evokes that same materiality, takes over – but can never replace it. While the light on the screen is absolutely regular (though we do not see them, the points are fixed in a permanent grid), no vibration or randomness of any sort is foreseen. An ever greater modulation in hues and contrast is possible, among other things, so that the screening can be personalised, giving complete freedom to the projectionist, yet *directors of photography* always fought to obtain copies of uniform colour quality from the laboratories. In the end, compared to cinema, digital cinema is something else, and that is that. Perhaps it is the only human conquest that has evolved in pursuit of technological perfection, and is now losing quality. We get used to everything[208] of course, and there will certainly be no drama as the change is gradual. But it will be up to cinema museums to teach the next generations how we were in the days of moving images.

208 As was the case for audio CDs, digital photography, and black and white photography which rendered the production of certain chemicals obsolete to the point of causing a crisis in the industry and the closure of many important plants.

Epilogue

This book was first published in Italian in 2006 and was reissued with an update in 2009.

Over the past 10 years technology has changed a lot in cinemas and an era has probably come to an end, yet to understand how the grammar and syntax of audiovisual language came into being it is important to start from the beginning as we have done here. I do not know if "digital cinema" can still be called cinema or if we ought to find another name for it. But the principles that underlie the combination of moving images and sound do not depend on the medium used.

The technological development of what we continue to call digital cinema is progressive, continuous and fast. When one element is perfected, adjustments are required throughout the chain of creation, production, distribution and access. This has a domino effect on equipment that today is identified as "professional" with a certain difficulty. In the meantime, the boundaries that strictly divided cinema from television until a couple of decades ago, have been superseded. Even in everyday language it has become difficult to establish a clear distinction between a *film camera* and a *video camera*.

Photographs, but also family videos are taken with smartphones; cameras now take high quality still images but also shoot film clips; video cameras now store their images on digital memory cards and have taken over from cine-cameras that used celluloid film.

There are some directors who still prefer to work with film, though as of 2012 *analogue* equipment is no longer produced. Christopher Nolan, in particular, continues to believe in it, to the point that after having shot *Dunkirk* (2017) in 35mm and IMAX, he released it in three celluloid formats (IMAX, 70mm and 35mm anamorphic) and three digital formats (IMAX laser, IMAX xenon and DCP).

This development began at the turn of the new millennium. Initially, it involved a physical dismantling of technological systems that had been perfected over the years in favour of the illusory nature of increasingly powerful computer-managed programmes. Applications have been enhanced over time, such as *motion capturing* used to replicate features or movements from real life, or *morphing* which can alter them. Many films no longer even need sets, as bodies or objects can be composited into any variety of backgrounds. Blue or green screens (red is not taken into consideration as it interacts with skin colour) can be wholly or partiality deleted from the composition with absolute precision by a multitude of technician, whose sheer number is just amazing, especially in more elaborate productions. The power and reliability of memory cards (dating from the late 1980s and in continuous development) have contributed to the miniaturisation of equipment for shooting and post-production. Machines on set are increasingly light and manageable thanks to aluminium alloys and ergonomic designs (the latest steadicams and drones), not to mention LED lights (Light Emitting Diode, 1962) which, though lighter and smaller, are more energy efficient, have adaptable colour temperature and are very powerful. In short, every sector is undergoing continuous evolution (which we hope is not an involution).

From the first DAC chip (1969, Bell laboratories), the race was on to simulate photographic quality in video and Sony was the front runner: the first HD F900 came out in 2000 (also known as Panavision HD-900F). Subsequently, other companies (starting with James Jannard's RED) aimed at increasing definition but also performance (slow motion), coming closer to the standards of analog cinema and even adopting its sophisticated lenses. Sensors have increased in potential and are currently at 8K (Red Epic W, Weapon 8KS35: 8192 x 4320 pixels) with an increasingly extended dynamic range, because, beyond definition, the limit remains precisely the range and therefore the overall quality of scalar relationship between white and black. This, then, turns out to be one of the points against digital when compared to celluloid.

While the options for filming at the moment are either celluloid, including wide gauge, or else continuous experimentation with the improving quality of the primary digital source (what we once would have called the negative), paradoxically, for the last two decades now (i.e. since celluloid has been banned from theatres – the first digital projections were in 1999) the standard in projection has been the 2K DCP (Digital Cinema Package). The same can be said for 3D cinema, which, since cinema began, returns periodically relaunched as a complete novelty (this time thanks to digital simulations that can create objects not used when shooting) and then disappears again because of issues experienced by spectators sitting to the sides of the theatre. So, reiterating that old catchphrase "in a few select theatres", used to promote Dolby Stereo, while unimaginable events can be viewed in those very few theatres equipped for IMAX projection, whether on celluloid, digital or laser, the industry cannot ignore digital platforms where the end user may be alone with their i-Phone (as NETFLIX has shown). Alone with miniaturised audio, while in the few surviving select "temples" of the image – even audio is perfected in computer processors – the spectator is immersed in 64-channel multidimensional Dolby Atmos. And in the meantime, the self-referential LED screen, which ought to make the video projector obsolete, has been announced.

Since the *telecine* has become a *scanner*, the criteria for archiving and managing films has also changed. In film restoration computer programmes (digital technology in general therefore) initially afforded great opportunities, importing images, reworking and/or restoring them and returning them to celluloid (as happened for special effects). Initially, the operation had an economic objective especially when dealing with more recent films, making them available for TV networks and the HOME VIDEO market, on laserdisc and then on DVD. But now, since theatres have been reconverted, these re-workings (often simple, accurate transcriptions, though the word "restoration" always sells) are an opportunity to create once unconceivable events (often programmed for one day only) dedicating the theatre and thus the large screen to an authentic masterpieces that would otherwise be confined to festivals and film archives. So, does digital also guarantee the preservation of films from the past? Unfortunately, No. As with "analogue" colour copies, there are still no secure systems for digital media. As research progresses, the equipment used for various decoding operations is also becoming obsolete. Progress itself means continuous change and consequent "recopying" to preserve data (in television alone, since the beginning of the 50s, there have been more than 40 video formats which have gradually become outdated). There has been only one format which has held its standard, though constantly perfected, since 1909: black & white celluloid film. It is still 35mm wide, the perforations have remained compatible, the support has been strengthened to become durable and even thinner (polyester), the emulsion needs only controlled temperature and humidity. It is to this format that we are examining the hypothesis of entrusting original digital products, DSM (Digital Source Master) data today stored on Linear Tape-Open supports. From silver, to pixel ... to silver, probably ... .

Index

Index

Index

NB. The index entries to footnotes (with suffix n*) are to the page numbers on which the note falls.*